The Teddy Bear Chronicles

HONG KONG LITERATURE SERIES
Series Editor: John Minford

The Teddy Bear Chronicles

by Xi Xi

Translated by
Christina Sanderson

The Chinese University of Hong Kong Press

HONG KONG LITERATURE SERIES
Series Editor: John Minford

The Teddy Bear Chronicles
By Xi Xi
Translated by Christina Sanderson

This new series of books, originally the brainchild of the prominent Hong Kong writer Leung Ping-kwan, proudly presents the defiant and distinctive character of Hong Kong's imaginative literature, which marks it off from the other parts of the Chinese-speaking world.

ISBN: 978-988-237-185-9

Published by:
The Chinese University of Hong Kong Press
The Chinese University of Hong Kong
Sha Tin, N.T., Hong Kong
Fax: +852 2603 7355
Email: cup@cuhk.edu.hk
Website: cup.cuhk.edu.hk

Printed in Hong Kong

Supported by 香港藝術發展局 Hong Kong Arts Development Council

Hong Kong Arts Development Council fully supports freedom of artistic expression. The views and opinions expressed in this project do not represent the stand of the Council.

Series Editor's Preface

From its first controversial founding as a British colony in 1842, Hong Kong has been a unique place of refuge for immigrants, protected from the turmoil of the Mainland, a haven in which this free-thinking, free-wheeling child of China's great literary culture has been able to survive and flourish, unimpeded by political struggle and the heavy hand of ideological dogma. In the tender core beneath this modern city's deceptively hard and glittering surface lies a world of fine literature, visual and performance art, music, theatre and film. It is one of the great civilised cities of the world. This new series of six books proudly presents that civilisation, giving evidence of the defiant and distinctive character of Hong Kong's imaginative literature, which marks it off from the other parts of the Chinese-speaking world. Like the better-known cinematic work of Wong Kar-wai, the literature of Hong Kong combines a timelessly Chinese palette of colours and flavours with an exciting acceptance of cosmopolitan modernity. It is as authentically Chinese as the very best Cantonese cuisine, and yet at the same time, having issued from a place which is so permeable and volatile, it is also infused with an effortless sense of fusion. It is an alchemy *of* Hong Kong, but *for* the world.

Liu Yichang, an immigrant from Shanghai in 1948, was for several decades, until his death in 2019 at the age of 99, the father figure of the modern Hong Kong literary scene. As editor of the journal *Hong Kong Literature*, he was widely respected for having nurtured younger talents such as Leung Ping-kwan and Xi Xi. His 1962 stream-of-consciousness novel *The Drunkard* vividly portrays the Hong Kong of the early 1960s, chronicling the struggle for survival in the jungle of the city of a dissolute but thoughtful and literate Chinese man of letters. It captures the quintessential spirit of Hong Kong, its magnificent, often squalid, splendour, its contradictions, its chaotic and irrepressible energy.

Leung Ping-kwan, who moved into Hong Kong with his parents from Guangdong Province as a small child in 1949, was a prolific and supremely gifted poet, critic, and writer of fiction. *Lotus Leaves* is the most complete anthology to date of translations from his poetic oeuvre, and shows the sheer range of his writing, from celebration of the everyday in Hong Kong life, to deeper meditations on the human condition, and playful pieces written for performance in the lively cultural scene in which he was so active a participant. His two tales in the companion volume *Dragons*, with their roots both in Latin-American Magical Realism and in the age-old Chinese tradition of tales of the supernatural, demonstrate his accomplishment as a storyteller.

Xi Xi also immigrated as a girl to Hong Kong from Shanghai, in 1950. Over the past five decades she has created a large and uniquely personal body of work, as a writer of both fiction and poetry. She is widely admired for her great stylistic elegance and for the poignant and haunting, almost melancholic, mood of much of her writing. *The*

Teddy Bear Chronicles is a quirky and original work, cleverly bringing together her passion for the making of teddy bears with a number of short essays about colourful figures from Chinese history. It is a charming album, both instructive and entertaining, leaving the reader with a feeling of pure delight.

The memoir *Ordinary Days* by the scholar and critic Leo Ou-fan Lee and his wife Esther brings to this series an intensely personal touch, consciously echoing that great sentimental memoir of the late 18th century, Shen Fu's *Six Chapters of a Floating Life*. With disarming candour, Leo and Esther lay bare their hearts and share with us their story of love and suffering. Set partly against the backdrop of some of Hong Kong's most turbulent years, partly in the far-flung diaspora of the Chinese intelligentsia, this is a remarkably revealing record of the inner life of a highly cultivated modern Chinese couple.

The Best China, an anthology of Hong Kong essays from the past 170 years, records the intellectual ferment that has always characterized the city, sometimes restless and questioning, sometimes meditative and lyrical, always civilised, and buoyed by an all-pervasive spirit of freedom.

To borrow from the title of one of Xi Xi's works, we could perhaps call this series *Six Chapters from a Floating City*: a tribute to the indomitable spirit of the people of the special world that is Hong Kong.

John Minford
March 5, 2020
Featherston, New Zealand

Acknowledgements

From 2013 this project was made possible by the generous logistical support of the Centre for China Studies, The Chinese University of Hong Kong. Especial thanks are due to its Director, Professor David Faure, and its Executive Officer, Ms Gillian Wu. Without their constant help and encouragement, and that of other members of the Centre (Professors Jan Kiely and John Lagerwey), I would have given up *years* ago.

In the autumn of 2012, a year after the 2011 Symposium at which the idea was first put forward by my friend PK, or to give him his full title, Professor Leung Ping-kwan, fifty or so graduate students at The Chinese University of Hong Kong enrolled in a semester-long course on translating Hong Kong Literature. Professor Leung came along towards the end of the semester and took part in an impromptu workshop at one of our seminars. He was already very ill, but his dedication to the cause of Hong Kong Literature always remained in the forefront of his mind, to his dying day. His talk that day inspired us all, and ultimately his passion has been the driving force behind this project.

Over the years many young translators have generously contributed their talents to the various books in the series, working from

Hong Kong, Australia, New Zealand, Canada, and the United States, inspired by a shared love of Hong Kong, a shared admiration for the spirit of the place, and a determination to show the world the depth and fascination of its literature and of its unique culture.

Finally, I wish to thank the enthusiastic and dedicated team at The Chinese University of Hong Kong Press. The Press Director Ms Gan Qi, and the Acquisitions Editor Ms Ye Minlei, welcomed the project with open arms, and over the past few months their editors 'on the ground', Ms Winifred Sin and Ms Rachel Pang, have toiled with enormous professionalism on some complex manuscripts. Throughout the often challenging process of bringing this project to fruition they have been a most congenial team to work with, many times expressing to me the pride they feel in helping to create this tribute to their city and its great tradition of freedom.

John Minford
June 2020

Contents

Preface

This introduction is partly inspired by an essay written by the Hong Kong critic Stephen C. Soong, which was published in Chinese in the *Ming Pao Monthly* for November 1985, and subsequently adapted and translated into English in 1986 for the first collection of Xi Xi's stories in translation, *A Girl Like Me and Other Stories*. Stephen Soong (1919–1996) was one of the first critics to recognise the importance of Xi Xi's work, and to promote it both in Hong Kong and in Taiwan.

Xi Xi is the pen name of the writer Cheung Yin. She was born in Shanghai in 1937 and settled in Hong Kong in 1950. Her family originally came from Zhongshan, in Guangdong Province. Xi Xi attended Heep Yunn School in Hong Kong and later entered the Grantham College of Education. After graduation she taught at a government primary school, before devoting herself full-time to writing.

In 1983, her short story *A Girl Like Me* won a prestigious prize in Taiwan, and since then she has been awarded numerous literary prizes for her fiction and her poetry, culminating in the 2019 Newman Prize for Chinese Literature, from the University of Oklahoma. In September 1989, she was admitted to hospital with cancer. She recovered after treatment, though repercussions impaired the use of her right hand. In recent years, Xi Xi has used her left hand to write. She has become very fond of doll houses and of making rag dolls and teddy bears by hand. This has served as physical therapy for her right hand.

Xi Xi, in its Chinese written form 西西, is a graphic representation, a pictograph, of a young girl in a skirt, her legs spread within a chalked frame, playing a game called 'Building a House', popular among young Chinese girls in Hong Kong. Her own account of her pen name was charmingly explained in a short essay of hers:

> *When I was young I used to love playing a game similar to hopscotch, which we called 'Building a House' or 'Aeroplane Hopping'. First you draw a series of squares on the ground. Then you tie a string of paper clips into a knot and toss it into one of the squares and start hopping from one square to the next until you reach the square with the knot in it. Then you pick it up and hop your way back to where you started. When I played this game with a lot of other children, I always found it exciting; sometimes I played it alone, and felt very lonely. When I was in primary school, I played it all the time. Now that I am a teacher, I still play with the children ...*

From this account we can learn something of Xi Xi's attitude toward life: she is a person of childlike joy. We can also see this particular game as a metaphor. The squares represent form or convention, and Xi Xi feels no sense of such restriction; she can jump from one square to the next as she pleases. Or they may be seen to represent the squares on the manuscript paper used by Chinese authors, the rules of the writing game Xi Xi the author has learned both to respect and disobey. As she herself says, 'crawling from square to square' (a standard Chinese metaphor for the process of writing) is a more painful exercise than hopscotch.

Xi Xi is very much a writer 'made in Hong Kong'. She regards children's tales, the cinema, and European and Latin American fiction as major influences. She has read most of Andersen's and Wilde's tales, and her works are permeated with a childlike quality. Perhaps this is the product of her years of teaching in a primary school, although she has never deliberately written for children, and her expressions of childish delight are often restrained. She confesses to having been influenced by Mario Vargas Llosa and Gabriel García Márquez, but her works are not in any sense transplants, they are thoroughly Chinese. She does not reject the Chinese tradition. She is essentially a cosmopolitan Chinese writer.

The delightful pieces in *The Teddy Bear Chronicles* belong to a long and venerable tradition in Chinese literature, of quirky memoirs and casual personal essays, sometimes lyrical, sometimes telling a story. These miniatures might record a distant memory, a fleeting dream, or some recent experience. They were often written around a theme that had exercised a particular fascination (sometimes an obsession) on their author: strange creatures, eccentric habits, unusual pastimes. This type of thing was called in Chinese the informal literature of 'jottings' (*biji wenxue*). The vast treasury of such work written in Chinese over the past two thousand years has been hugely neglected outside the Chinese world. This is because it fits so awkwardly, if at all, into any existing Western category. It is quintessentially Chinese, and for that very reason very hard to translate. Like a knick-knack from the studio of a Chinese man of letters, some exquisitely carved walnut stone, or small personal seal with a brief and tantalising inscription engraved by the owner's friend, the *biji* essay creates around itself a leisurely world of its own. It projects a view of the world in which things (sometimes the tiniest things) are brought into sharp but effortless focus. It reflects a refined and deeply (but lightly) philosophical aesthetic, that goes back as far as the great Taoist raconteur Master Zhuang of the fourth century BC (needless to say, Xi Xi made a teddy of him!). To read his essays is to partake of the deeply illogical magic of things Chinese. It is to be both entertained and enlightened. Xi Xi's bear-essays are a superb and exquisite modern re-incarnation of this form. With their accompanying photographic illustrations, they transport us to a private universe, made the more poignant by the circumstances of its creation (in the aftermath of cancer). Her great skill as a writer, combine with her gently zany sense of humour and a touch of whimsy, to take us on a light-hearted trip through Chinese history and culture—not for some heavy educational purpose, but for pure pleasure. Fortunately for readers with no knowledge of Chinese, Xi Xi and her teddy bears have found a truly sensitive soul-mate in Christina Sanderson, a gifted young translator who has herself come to 'know their sound', and has dedicated herself to bringing these lovable creatures out into the world.

John Minford
March 2020
Featherston, New Zealand

Chinese Bears in Antique Garb

with introductory notes added by the translator

Legendary Times
(c.2100–c.1600 BC)

The Queen Mother of the West, Yi the Archer and Chang'e

The Queen Mother of the West is a legendary being in Chinese mythology, supposed to dwell upon the Kunlun Mountains and to have been visited there by King Mu of Zhou. In her garden grow the famous peaches which ripen but once in 3,000 years and confer immortality upon those who eat them. Later tradition has given her a husband called the Royal Lord of the East.[1]

Hou Yi, or simply 'Yi', is the famed heroic archer said to have rescued humans from imminent annihilation. He shot down nine (or in some texts ten) surplus suns which once rose together and scorched the earth. He was given the elixir of immortality by the Queen Mother of the West as a reward, but his wife, Chang'e, stole it and flew away to the moon. She would become the Goddess of the Moon.[2]

According to the ancient *Book of Hills and Seas*, 'The Queen Mother of the West is a half-goddess, half-beast mountain sprite dwelling in the Kunlun Mountains, with tiger teeth and a leopard tail, who is a good whistler.' Such was the depiction of the Queen Mother of the West during the Warring States period. Famous Chinese writers like Qu Yuan, Zhuangzi, and Xunzi all made mention of her. Xunzi went so far as to claim that she was the teacher of

1 Based on Herbert Allen Giles, *A Chinese Biographical Dictionary* (Leyden: Brill, 1898), p. 272.

2 Yang Lihui and An Deming, *Handbook of Chinese Mythology* (Santa Barbara: ABC-CLIO, 2005), pp. 231–232.

Emperor Yu the Great. By the Han Dynasty she had begun to be portrayed in a rather lavish style, as a beautiful woman. According to this era, she used to meet King Mu of Zhou down by the Jasper Lake, where they would sing ritual songs to one another. By the Wei, Jin, and Southern and Northern Dynasties, she had come to represent Taoist immortality.

The reason why the Queen Mother of the West is so famous and venerated is because she is the goddess in charge of administering the elixir of life. The stone relief portraits found in Han Dynasty tombs depict her alongside immortal Taoist priests, and a special rabbit, which helped to pound up the elixir. Besides these, she had two other capable followers in tow: a three-legged bird and a nine-tailed fox. Despite the many changes to the way in which she was depicted over the centuries, one thing has remained the same, and by it she is easily identified. It is the distinctive crown she wears upon her head. This crown came to symbolise the divine authority of the Queen Mother of the West. Later, it became a fashion accessory for ordinary girls. It is round in the middle, with two triangles placed above and below the circle, pointing in towards one another. A pair of these is set suspended at either end of a horizontal rod, which together make a complete crown. There are gold, silver, jade, silk, and coloured paper crowns, as well as brocade and floral designs. During the Wei, Jin, and Southern and Northern Dynasties, floral crowns were exchanged as lucky talismans on Humans' Day, celebrated on the seventh day of the first month each year. The crown I fashioned for my Queen Mother of the West is a pearl variation. She is wearing a short-sleeve coat over her robe.

The clothes and accessories 'worn' by the Queen Mother of the West in the Han relief portraits were drawn according to the contemporary trends of the Han Dynasty. Classical Chinese clothing stems from two main traditions: one involves a two-piece set that began in the Shang and Zhou

Dynasties made up of a shirt and a skirt. This later developed into a two-piece set comprising of a short jacket with a long robe underneath. The other main tradition stemmed from a one-piece: a shirt or blouse sewn on to a skirt. This started to gain popularity during the Warring States period (others say these one-pieces were already around in the Zhou Dynasty) and remained in fashion up until the Han Dynasty. The well-known long, unlined gowns for men, and the wrap-around dresses for women of later ages all developed down this line. Han Chinese clothing began with the shirt and skirt two-piece combination and was followed by many different kinds of one-pieces that appeared later. Every change in trend through the ages is actually attributable to the impact of foreign fashion on China.

As for Yi the Archer and his wife Chang'e, their story is one we all know well. I tailored a piece of leather for Yi to wear as a skirt. The name of his skirt comes from the early period. The sides of the skirt were not supposed to be sewn up. Chang'e is wearing a knife-pleat 'hundred fold' skirt, with a floaty chiffon wrap around her shoulders to give extra movement. Skirts in the Han Dynasty were a single piece of material wrapped around the waist like a tube.

Yi is carrying a bow and arrows. The arrows were stored on his back in a quiver called a *fu*, which were usually made out of bamboo or cane. One of these quivers could hold up to ten arrows. The arrows were bundled with the tips pointing downwards, and the feathers and shafts poking out of the top. By the Tang Dynasty, the name *fu* had changed to *hulu*, which by then referred to a pouch slung from a large belt worn around the waist. One *hulu* could hold thirty arrows. A *hulu* made from wild boar hide was used to sound out invading enemy troops. It was claimed that a scout who crouched down and rested his head on a *hulu* placed on the ground could detect sounds of movement up to thirty miles away.

Legendary Times
(c.2100–c.1600 BC)

The Yellow Emperor and Leizu

The Yellow Emperor is one of the most famous of China's legendary rulers. He is said to have reigned 2698–2598 BC, and to have been miraculously conceived by his mother Fu Bao, who gave birth to him on the banks of the Ji River, from which he took his surname, Ji. His personal name was Youxiong, taken from that of his hereditary Principality; and also Xuanyuan, said by some to be the name of a village near which he dwelt, by others to refer to wheeled vehicles of which he was traditionally the inventor, as well as being the inventor of armour, ships, pottery, and other useful appliances. The close of his long reign was made glorious by the appearance of the phoenix and the mysteriously auspicious animal known as the *qilin* (commonly misrepresented in English as the 'Chinese Unicorn'), in token of his wise and humane administration. He died at the age of 111 years.

Xiling Shi, the Lady of Xiling (after her birthplace in Hubei Province) was a title given to Leizu, consort of the Yellow Emperor. She is said to have discovered and taught the art of rearing silkworms in the 27th century BC.[3]

The Yellow Emperor's surname was Gongsun. His given name was Xuanyuan; according to some this was because he was born on the hillock of Xuanyuan. As he grew up on the banks of the Ji River, he had another surname, Ji. The Yellow Emperor was the leader of the nomadic Youxiong clan and various other neighbouring tribes. His greatest achievement was to

3 Based on Giles, *A Chinese Biographical Dictionary*, pp. 338 and 270.

take an extremely clever woman called Leizu for his wife. Leizu was the daughter of the chief of the Xiling tribe, who lived nearby the present-day Xiling Gorge in Sichuan Province. She was obviously an exceptionally creative person. It was she who discovered that natural silk could be derived from the cocoons silkworms produce after eating mulberry leaves, and that silk could then be woven into fabric for making clothes. She was first adopted by the head of the clan as a daughter, and later became the head of the clan herself. The entire clan was occupied in raising silkworms, spinning silk, and weaving cloth, which brought prosperity and the ability to expand out across the Chengdu Plain. When we say that the Yellow Emperor 'took' Leizu as a wife, it actually means that he married into Leizu's family, since theirs was a matriarchal society.

For her to grasp the process of raising silk worms and reeling silk was a truly amazing feat. It was no less than the beginning of Chinese clothing culture, the point from which China was able to break away from barbarism. The entire history of clothing in China began with Leizu. Her technique for rinsing silk floss later contributed to the invention of paper and printing.

Women in ancient China were largely occupied picking mulberry leaves. The indispensable tool required for this task was not a regular basket, but a flat, bamboo carrier called a *long*. These were very attractive objects. The Han Dynasty ballad *The Mulberry Leaves by the Path* is about a woman called Luo Fu taking up one such container to go picking mulberry leaves:

Fastened with black hair,
Cassia twigs for a handle …

The straps holding the *long* together were woven from strands of women's hair, and the handle was made from cassia twigs or branches. These 'cassia twigs' are actually what we now know as cinnamon bark, a kind of fragrant wood. In the ballad, cassia is used to represent Luo Fu's noble and unsullied character.

Leizu lived long, long ago in remote antiquity, and as such, she wouldn't have been as particular about her clothes as those who came after her. My Leizu bear is wearing a simple smock with an apron tied around it. She is fairly rich, as you can tell by looking at her necklace, which is made of cowry shells, the currency of her time.

When the Yellow Emperor took his people to live with him in Sichuan, he merged the Youxiong and Xiling tribes to form a single large clan. This represented the end of their nomadic existence: they had entered the Agricultural Era. The Yellow Emperor stayed in Chengdu for two years, where two sons were born to him. He then returned to the Central Plain and defeated Chiyou, the tyrannical leader of the Nine Li tribe. This victory united the rest of the disparate tribes in the region. Their social system changed from matriarchy to patriarchy. At that time, clothing started to become more fancy and dignified. Prior to the Yellow Emperor's unification of the tribes, there were no set styles when it came to clothes. I designed this outfit for him. The upper garment imitates the one-shoulder tunics popular in the Bronze Age, as found at the famous archaeological site at Sanxingdui in Sichuan. The thing joined to it is a bunch-pleat, or 'gathered' skirt. All the emperors of later ages, from the Song, to the Yuan, Ming, and Qing Dynasties loved to wear these roomy gathered skirts.

Shang Dynasty
(c.1600–c.1028 BC)

Lady Fu Hao

Fu Hao (d.1200 BC) was one of the many wives of King Wu Ding of the Shang Dynasty. Unusually for the time, she also served as a military general and high priestess. Her treasure-filled tomb was discovered and excavated in 1976, not far from the Shang capital Yinxu, within what is today the city of Anyang.

Lady Fu Hao was the first great heroine of ancient China. Legend has it that the most important contribution was made by the Yellow Emperor's wife, Leizu, as the inventor of sericulture. But whether she actually existed or not remains uncertain to this day. There is no such question about Fu Hao. Fu Hao was the lawfully wedded wife of the Shang Dynasty king, Wu Ding. Even though she was just the queen consort, she nevertheless had her own territory, land, and private armed forces. She was a general and as such would often assist her husband by leading troops into battle. Fu Hao and Wu Ding used to join forces to defend the nation. Wu Ding had many wives and concubines, but Fu Hao appears to have been his favourite. She would often take up the duties of the master of ceremonies at sacrificial rites, and would deliver the formal elegy. As the official diviner, she was able to interpret the oracle inscriptions on tortoise shells and animal bones, which in the days of remote antiquity was no simple task. By virtue of being so well-versed in both civil and military affairs, Fu Hao became known as a person of all-round accomplishments.

Unfortunately, Fu Hao passed away when she was in her thirties. Perhaps she died from injuries sustained in war, or complications during childbirth. Fu Hao's son was the Prince Xiao Ji. In his later years,

Wu Ding gradually began to lose his mind. Believing the slander that had been laid against his son to be true, he sent the prince (a son who by all accounts was very filial indeed) into exile. Xiao Ji finally died in mysterious circumstances. Immeasurable grief ensued across the land. At least Fu Hao did not have to bear witness to the tragedy that befell her son, since she had long since been in her resting place at Anyang, in present-day Henan Province.

In recent years, Lady Hao's tomb has been unearthed. It was found to be a veritable treasure trove, containing: exquisitely crafted bronze ritual vessels and weapons (468 pieces), jade ware (over 590 pieces), cowries (over 6,000 pieces), hairpins and accessories (500 pieces), and bone artifacts (560 pieces). In addition there were ivory goods, earthenware, silks and linens, a large Arabian cowry, and two veined rapa whelks.

All of these were precious rarities in ancient China.

In her tomb Fu Hao herself was adorned with jade. The four great 'pillars' of Chinese civilization were considered to be jade, lacquer, silk, and porcelain; bronze was not included, as it was to be found all over the world. Jade, on the other hand, was extremely rare in ancient times (though the Mayans of Mexico and Maori tribes of New Zealand also had it). No ancient civilisation attached as much importance to jade as the Chinese, or had as many uses for it. In China, jade has

long been a beautiful symbol of good luck and happiness, with the power to connect man to the gods. It never deteriorates. The word jade has come into common usage in Chinese, found in phrases like 'jade perfection', 'jade beauty' and 'jade girl'. The item attracting the most attention among those unearthed from Fu Hao's tomb was her large bronze battle-axe, which features her memorial inscription. This axe, which was an emblem of her royal prowess, weighs nine kilograms. As a matter of fact, when unearthed from her tomb, even the bronze

sacrificial vessels were found to be 'wearing clothes', as remnants of silk fibres were discovered on the surfaces.

I gave my Fu Hao bear this scarf to make her look like an ancient priestess. The material was a present given to me by a friend. She bought it as a souvenir from the National Palace Museum in Taipei. The design is taken from inscriptions on the ancient bronze San-family Bowl, which some have claimed contain details about a contract for the transfer of ownership of land, said to have been bought by the San family from another noble clan. The bowl explains how both parties would use certain mountains, rivers, roads, and trees as border markers to divide their respective portions of land. A notary public is even mentioned in the inscription, proving that even in antiquity there already existed such a thing as privately-owned land. Another explanation maintains that the inscriptions referred to a dispute between two vassal states under the jurisdiction of the Shang king. According to this second explanation, the bowl outlines a treaty due to come into effect after the king ordered the aggressors to return the disputed land. The 'bowl' in question was actually a type of bronze basin used for holding water. It came with a gourd-shaped scoop. These were actually quite like the water pitchers and basins used by the Western nobility for washing their faces. The decorations on the sides of the vessel use the 'beast-face mask' motif. As people in the Shang Dynasty used to style their hair in plaits and braids, I decided to give Fu Hao a long plait here.

Spring and Autumn
(722–481 BC)

Fan Li and Xi Shi

Fan Li (b.517 BC) was a military adviser in the southern feudal State of Yue. He is famous for planning the scheme whereby his master, King Goujian, was enabled to reduce the rival State of Wu. It was Fan Li who found the great beauty Xi Shi and sent her as a 'gift' to Fuchai, the King of Wu. After this success he withdrew from official life, declaring that Goujian was one with whom adversity but not prosperity might be shared; and that having spent the best part of his life in the public service, he wished to devote his remaining energies to private enjoyment. Xi Shi (506 BC– ?) would become one of the renowned 'Four Beauties' of ancient China. As the story goes, if Xi Shi leaned over a balcony to look at the fish in a pond, the fish would be so dazzled by her beauty that they would forget to swim and sink lifeless to the bottom.[4]

Fan Li and Xi Shi were both southerners. Fan Li hailed from the State of Chu. Xi Shi was from the State of Yue, in the area around present day Shaoxing, Zhejiang Province. At the end of the Spring and Autumn Period, the customs and habits of dress of the southern States of Wu and Yue were completely different from those seen in the Central Plain. People of the

4 Based on Giles, *A Chinese Biographical Dictionary*, p. 217.

Central Plain let their hair grow from birth. Once it had grown long enough they would wind it up into a bun and put on either a hairpin, headband, or head cloth, or cover it with a hat. Yue people would cut their hair short. They had tattoos as well. In general, short hair and tattoos stemmed from totem worship. Their tattoos were simple pictures of certain plants and animals. They signified the bearer's particular clan, and served as a source of protection. Besides this, they were a form of cosmetic beauty, like makeup. Come to think of it, Xi Shi—the so-called 'Wise Beauty'—would have been very unlikely to go against the customs of her day, though none of the portraits throughout history depict her with short hair or tattoos.

Xi Shi and Fan Li are wearing typical ethnic clothes, colourful and made of cotton, which would distinguish them from the tribes of the north. They are nevertheless still composed of a shirt on top and a skirt below with a belt tied around the waist. I cut and combed the head of hair I made for Fan Li into a high, short ponytail. This style was later taken up by the Japanese and eventually became the now famous hair-style of the ronin and samurai.

In his management of strategic and economic affairs, Fan Li possessed an extraordinary talent rarely seen in history. Most exceptionally, he had both the courage to advance and the courage to retreat. To advance is always easy; the difficult aspect of strategy lies rather in mastering a timely withdrawal. I've made him wear an embroidered stole in bright ethnic colours across his shoulders. Both Xi Shi and Fan Li are in simple smocks. Xi Shi is also wearing a belt from which waist pendants could be hung. She has a butterfly comb in her hair; these have been very popular with girls for centuries. By the Tang Dynasty, a hairdo could feature more than ten of these combs.

Warring States
(403–221 BC)

Zhong Lichun

Zhong Lichun, who was also called Zhong Wuyan, went down in history for two things: her unsightly appearance and her sage advice. She lived in the 4th century BC.

In the time of the Warring States, in the north-eastern State of Qi (part of present-day Shandong), in the town of Wuyan, there lived an ugly woman named Zhong Lichun. Everyone thought it funny to call her Zhong 'Wuyan', instead of her real given name, Lichun, because besides being the name of her hometown, *wuyan* also happens to mean 'unattractive'. She had a sunken forehead, long squinting eyes, hardly any hair, an upturned nose, and a prominent Adam's apple. She was also stooped over, with sagging breasts and a dark, leathery complexion. When she was already forty years old there was still no husband in sight.

One day, Zhong Wuyan went to see King Xuan of Qi and declared that the state of Qi was facing four grave crises. Her frank advice moved the king deeply. He not only implemented her suggested reforms, but proceeded to take her as his wife. And so she became queen. For a common, unattractive woman to be received by a monarch, to express her political views, and then have them endorsed is an extremely rare occurrence, even by the standards of the democracies of today. What makes Zhong's situation all the more intriguing is that the king then decided to marry her.

This was not the first time in history that a Chinese monarch had married an ugly, virtuous woman. The Yellow Emperor married an unsightly, yet virtuous woman called Momu after Leizu passed away. In the later Three Kingdoms period, there was another such case, involving a famous southern scholar called Huang Chengyan. As the story goes, one day Huang approached the famous strategic wizard Zhuge Liang,[5] saying, 'I've heard you're seeking a wife, sir. I've got a girl. She's not much to look at; with hair bleached by the sun and

5 Zhuge Liang (181–234) is recognised as the most accomplished strategist of the Three Kingdoms era. He was born in Shandong and served as the Chancellor and Regent of the State of Shu.

a swarthy complexion. But she's every bit as clever as you are.' Zhuge Liang expressed his approval, whereupon Huang had his daughter delivered in a carriage to be wed.

When all's awry
Trust in the ugly Zhong Wuyan;
When all's well in the world
Turn to your beautiful queen.

Or so the saying goes.

In plays and stories, Zhong Wuyan is portrayed as an extremely talented and versatile woman. She, too, like Fu Hao, seems to have been a mistress of matters civil and martial; capable of waging war, solving diplomatic issues, and once even of untying her hands from behind her back. In one instance she saved the day by being able to play a special instrument with lotus root threads for strings. On stage she is always portrayed with split-face makeup. For her teddy bear I used purple mohair and gave her a blue butterfly shaped patch as an accessory. She should look plain and simple, but I think some bright colours are in order for a queen, don't you?

In the Spring and Autumn Period and throughout the Warring States, so far as women's headwear was concerned, hairpins called *ji* were all the rage. They are distinctly visible in Han Dynasty stone relief portraits. According to records about these hairpins from the Eastern Han Dynasty, queens were supposed to have worn six of them set in a high bun, just as it says in *The Book of Songs*:

Together forever, my Lord and I
Six jewelled pins in my hair ...

Later in history, the name for hairpin changed from *ji* to *zan*. Six pins should suffice for an ugly queen like Zhong Wuyan.

The monstrosity to her right is actually a proper headdress, a *jingguo*, which was a popular kind of wig at the time. Why wear a wig? For beauty's sake, of course! A wig can be loaded up with all sorts of pearls and sparkling jewels. Another benefit of a wig is that if you're in a hurry, you can put it on in one go just like a hat, and not have to spend time doing your hair. Since these wigs were exclusively worn by women, the meaning of the word *jinguo* eventually extended to become a fixed term referring to women. That is precisely what Zhuge Liang (he who allegedly had no qualms about marrying an ugly lady ...) meant when he once sent one as a 'present' to his opponent Sima Yi, who had decided to shut himself behind closed doors instead of going out to fight. The female wig was a taunt sent to ridicule Sima for his reluctance to attack. Mr Zhuge must have forgotten that many of the 'wigs'

of the world are just as brave as the 'beards'. The first great general in China's recorded history was Fu Hao, who was, of course, a woman.

I found an interesting wig for my Zhong Wuyan bear. It looks like the old hairdo of the Dutch soccer star Ruud Gullit. Zhong Wuyan is wearing a short jacket on top and a long skirt below. This kind of two-piece outfit was identical for men and women. The only difference was that men wore their skirts outside their jackets. No matter whether you were a man or a woman, everybody wore skirts in those days.

Warring States
(403–221 BC)

Master Zhuang

Zhuang Zhou (3rd and 4th cent. BC) commonly known as Zhuangzi, 'Master Zhuang', was a native of Meng in modern Anhui, who devoted his life and energies to the glorification of Laozi. When the Prince of Chu, hearing of his fame as a scholar, sent messengers with costly gifts to offer him the post of Prime Minister, Zhuangzi smiled and said, 'You offer me great wealth and a proud position indeed; but have you ever seen a sacrificial ox? After being fattened up for several years it is decked with embroidered trappings and led to the altar; but would it not then willingly change places with some uncared-for pigling? ... Begone! I will never take office.' He accordingly gave himself up entirely to the study of philosophy, attacking the schools of Confucius and Mozi with such dialectic skill that the best scholars of the age were unable to refute his destructive criticism. He is traditionally credited as the author of at least part of the work bearing his name, the *Zhuangzi*.[6]

Master Zhuang was a fascinating individual. He seems to have had more stories up his sleeve than anybody else in the world. Some are long, others are short; but they're all utterly absorbing and wonderfully imaginative. They're also full of paradoxes—to use a favourite expression of his (even though it's become a bit of a *cliché*). In one instance, a gigantic bird capable of flying ninety thousand miles in one flap of the wing turns out to be the transformation of a miniscule fish. In another, a massive gourd

6 For an excellent translation see Burton Watson, *The Complete Works of Zhuangzi* (New York: Columbia University Press, 1968).

that was hopeless as a jug makes an excellent sailing boat. Then there's that huge, useless tree, which delights in being considered useless. Since nobody wants it for anything, it can come to no harm. Why wouldn't it be happy about that?

The founder of the study of aesthetics in modern China, Zhu Guangqian, once wrote an essay discussing three different perspectives for looking at ancient pine trees. It's interesting enough. But aeons before this, Master Zhuang had already introduced another, completely different point of view: that of the tree itself. Once we can imagine a tree with its own point of view, we won't go around thinking ourselves better than trees, or imposing our will upon them. From then on, we will respect trees. Starting from a sense of respect for trees, we can go on to respect other things.

Master Zhuang is constantly teaching us how to see things differently: from the opposite angle; from the contrary point of view. The idea is to reveal how not to be stuck in our ideas, biased, or prejudiced. In one case, he asks: How can a summer-born bug whose life spans but a single season, ever hope to understand ice or snow? He goes on to explain why the summer bug has no way of understanding such things. It should be aware of its limitations, and accept the possibility of other points of view. It shouldn't go around judging things related to other seasons from its limited perspective as a summer bug. Humans perpetuate the mistake of the summer-born bug, and have done for more than two thousand years.

They say that a certain monarch once offered Master Zhuang the post of Prime Minister. He refused. Now that is an earnest renouncement of fame and fortune. His stories were certainly not idle chit-chat. He practised what he preached.

Sometimes Master Zhuang himself becomes the protagonist of his stories. The most famous is about a dream he once dreamed. He dreamed of a butterfly, then imagined himself as the butterfly; in the end he no longer knew for sure whether he was Master Zhuang dreaming of a butterfly, or a butterfly dreaming of a man called Zhuang. It has to be the best dream in history. When did we stop having wonderful dreams like that? Since when did our dreams become mere objects of psychopathology?

My Master Zhuang bear is most likely dreaming of butterflies in his sleep, too. You'll see he has a *wawa* pillow, with a doll's face at either end. Where is he sleeping? Under a big tree? On the grass? Like a butterfly, he is sleeping perched on a hedge.

Warring States
(403–221 BC)

Qu Yuan and the Mountain Spirit

Qu Yuan (c.340–278 BC) is still famous in China for his poetry and loyalty as a minister. He served in high office and enjoyed the full confidence of his sovereign until he was impeached through the intrigues of rivals. Then he composed the well-known poem entitled 'Falling into Trouble', which is an allegorical description of the writer's search for a prince who will listen to good counsels in government.[7] The elaborate 'rhapsody' (*fu*) poetic form would later develop from this. On the fifth day of the fifth lunar month Qu Yuan committed suicide by wading into a river holding a rock. Popular legend has it that local villagers rowed out and desperately tried to save him. To keep fish and evil spirits away from his body, they beat drums, splashed the water with their paddles and threw rice into the water to lure the fish away from his body. This was the origin of the annual Dragon Boat Festival, which commemorates Qu Yuan to this day.[8]

The 'Mountain Spirit' in Qu Yuan's *Nine Songs* collection of poems is a beautiful, mountain-dwelling sprite who glances and smiles at people. In her heart there is a lover for whom she yearns day and night, though she can never set eyes on him. In actual fact, the 'Mountain Spirit' is an incarnation of Qu Yuan himself. They are one-in-two, two-in-one.

7 Translated by David Hawkes as 'On Encountering Trouble', in John Minford and Joseph S. M. Lau eds., *Classical Chinese Literature: An Anthology of Translations* (Hong Kong: The Chinese University Press, 2000), pp. 240–253.

8 Based on Giles, *A Chinese Biographical Dictionary*, pp. 200–201.

Thinking of his love,

Standing alone in sadness.[9]

The poet-official Qu Yuan is our earliest ancestor of symbolism. In his thinking he went far beyond his time. In his poetry, sometimes he is transformed into a fragrant flower-like beauty, sometimes into a hermaphrodite. At other times he becomes an orange. Sometimes he addresses profound questions to Heaven.

My Mountain Spirit is covered all over with fur, tangled in a few artificial vines and flowers, of course. Both she and Qu Yuan are entwined with herbage. Qu Yuan was from the southern State of Chu, a creative, romantic region, the Chinese artistic centre of its day. Qu Yuan himself explained that his love for eccentric clothes began in childhood and carried on undiminished into maturity. That is why I've created this flamboyant suit for him, made up of a shirt sewed onto a skirt.

There are quite a few different kinds of these one-piece suits. This particular one worn by Qu Yuan is embellished with overlapping waves along the bottom hem, which reveal the coloured stripes of his inner garment. In ancient China both men and women wore skirts, as trousers had not yet been invented. Despite China's reputation as one of the great civilisations as far as clothing is concerned, the conservative strain has always been very strong. Qu Yuan's contemporary, King Wuling of Zhao, introduced clothing from the Hu ethnic minority. This transformed everyday wear from the long Han Dynasty robes to short jackets with narrow sleeves. It also brought about the common wearing of boots. Both of these new trends were better suited to horse riding and archery. Despite the fact that the new style made the nation stronger, there was nevertheless something about it that the conservative nobility found repellent. Their abhorrence of such clothes lay dormant until the king lost power, when it finally erupted.

Qu Yuan's eccentric clothes must have offended the eyes of many. But what was actually eccentric about them? Strange clothes were, after all, just one aspect of his eccentric behaviour. In such topsy-turvy times as his, if one didn't conform to popular trends in any way, one was already considered an eccentric.

At my belt a long sword swinging[10]

Qu Yuan's sword was a long and very beautiful object. As it was classified as an ornament, it would have been worn at the front. I couldn't find a real one for the bear, so I've substituted a chopstick. It has colourful *cloisonné* enamel decorations on it. Pretty nice, huh?

Qu Yuan mentioned that he used to wear some kind of tall headdress (*guan*), but I really don't know what that looked like. If it was a *guan* as worn in the Han Dynasty, then it was clearly one of the ones with tilted boards. I thought it best to let the poet go freely, humming along the riverbank with his hair loose.

---

9 Translated by David Hawkes, in Minford and Lau eds., *Anthology*, p. 262.

10 Translated by David Hawkes as 'On Encountering Trouble', quoted from Minford and Lau eds., *Anthology*, pp. 240–253. Please see also David Hawkes, *The Songs of the South: An Ancient Chinese Anthology of Poems by Qu Yuan and Other Poets* (Harmondsworth, Middlesex, England: Penguin Books Ltd, 1985), almost half of the poems of which are ascribed to Qu Yuan.

Warring States (403–221 BC)

Jing Ke and Gao Jianli

Jing Ke and Gao Jianli are famous in Chinese history for their respective attempts to assassinate the King of the State of Qin, Qin Shi Huang, who would survive to become China's First Emperor (r.221–210 BC). The events took place in the year 227 BC and are recorded in chapter 86, 'Biographhies of the Assassin-Retainers' of the *Records of the Grand Historian* by Sima Qian.[11]

The wind howls, xiao xiao,
The Yi River's cold.
Brave men, once gone,
Never come back again.

These were the lines of Jing Ke's tragic song which he sang as he set out to assassinate King Zheng of Qin, later to be become the First Emperor, Qin Shi Huang. He sang along with his friend Gao Jianli, a musician who sent him on his way with some taps on his bamboo lute. Jing failed in his attempt to assassinate the king, but that wasn't the end of the story. The Grand Historian Sima Qian added further lyrics to the song, as though Jing hadn't quite finished it, as though the melancholy music was still lingering on the wind.

Following Jing Ke's failed assassination attempt, the King of Qin deployed forces to hunt down any remaining rebels. To conceal himself, Gao Jianli changed his name and went into hiding, working as a servant in a tavern. But at the end of the day he was an artist, with music in his soul. Whenever he came across music that was

11 For a translation by Burton Watson, see 'Jing Ke, Assassin', in Minford and Lau eds., *Anthology*, pp. 341–351.

especially good or bad, it would reverberate in the depths of his being. Sure enough, the day came when he could restrain himself no longer. He let slip a few words of appreciation during a musical performance, which revealed his true identity. He gave up all efforts to conceal himself.

Recognising his worth, however, the King of Qin decided to spare his life, but blinded him. Gao was ordered to give lute recitals on demand. In so doing, he managed to gain the tyrant's trust, and eventually found a way to get close to him. In the darkness he fastened a heavy piece of lead to his lute, with which he hoped to strike the king dead. He would have but one chance to avenge his friend's death.

Sadly, despite his acute sense of hearing, he was completely blind, and his efforts came to nothing. We might consider Jing a professional assassin who unfortunately failed to master the essential skills of a swordsman. But Gao was more like a musical genius who ended up becoming a martyr by force of circumstance.

The Crown Prince of Yan and others who had knowledge of Jing Ke's plot to kill the king had lined the banks of the Yi River to bid him farewell when he set out. From head to toe they wore white, the colour of mourning. I made light chiffon clothes for the two martyr bears. Their outfits are similar; both have short jackets and long skirts, but the sleeves are different. When sitting cross-legged people preferred slightly narrower sleeve cuffs as these were better suited to instrumental playing; people who had to stand tended to wear wide, puffy 'lantern' sleeves, which gathered in to narrow cuffs. Robes featuring these cuffs were called *pao*, shirts without them were called *shan*.

Gao Jianli's instrument, the *zhu*, is a tapped lute or zither made of bamboo, which looks like a smaller version of the much larger *zheng*.

I had to use a *zheng* for the bear here because I couldn't find a toy *zhu*. When played, the *zhu* is held at its end by the left hand, while the right hand taps on the strings with a bamboo ruler.

The song Jing Ke sang about the Yi River is said to have modulated from a certain note of the ancient heptatonic scale to another note of the pentatonic scale. In other words, it changed from sounding mournful in the opening to sounding heroic by the end.

The Grand Historian's account of this episode is wonderfully vivid and gripping. Everyone involved knew (those who went to send Jing Ke off, and the martyr himself who was being sent off), that the enterprise was doomed to failure from the outset and that he was fated to die. His chances of success were minute. The words of Jing Ke's song blended with the natural setting to predict the ultimate failure of his enterprise.

Han Dynasty
(206 BC–AD 220)

Sima Xiangru and Zhuo Wenjun

The poet Sima Xiangru (c.179–117 BC) is generally regarded as the greatest composer of the rhapsody (*fu*) style of poetry in Chinese history. His meeting with Zhuo Wenjun provides an interesting twist on 'love at first sight'.

There once lived a gifted young man from Sichuan called Sima Xiangru. Besides being a talented poet, he was also a brilliant performer on the zither. One evening, he was giving a recital at the home of the wealthy iron manufacturer Zhuo Wangsun, and his playing reached the ears of his music-loving daughter, Wenjun, who had recently been widowed. From the moment she heard this music, she fell completely in love with him. Eventually, the pair eloped. The father was so furious that he refused to give his daughter a single cent. The

couple were obliged to open a small tavern to make ends meet. This 'golden girl' from the upper class was reduced to serving drinks as a common barmaid, while her lover joined the servants washing the cups in the kitchen, wearing a pair of 'calf-nose' shorts (*dubi kun*). *Kun* are simply shorts or trousers. These so-called calf-nose shorts were just about as short as shorts can be. In shape they were a bit like present-day baby nappies—they would have looked totally shabby and undignified.

Were they really so poor that he had to wear clothes like that? I would say they were in fact small-business people of their time. They certainly would have been too well-off to qualify for any kind of social security in Hong Kong these days. It seems likely that Sima Xiangru would have worn the shorts deliberately, to provoke his father-in-law, rather than out of genuine poverty. His scruffy appearance undoubtedly succeeded in infuriating the tycoon, for whom the whole affair represented a major loss of face. Utterly humiliated and seeing no alternative, Zhuo *père* sent a hundred servants and a million in copper cash to his daughter's household. The couple then moved to Chengdu, Sima Xiangru's old hometown, where they bought farmland and property, and lived in affluence.

Surprisingly, calf-nose shorts became something of a trend throughout the region. They must have spread to Japan, as you can still see them being worn by sumo wrestlers today. There's another story about these shorts set in the later period of the Wei-Jin Dynasties, in a village called Yuan. Yuan was split into two parts; all the rich families resided in the north, and all the poor families in the south. In the seventh lunar month of each year, the village would take part in a traditional ritual known as 'Sunning the Clothes'. Families in the north would flaunt their magnificent vestments outside in a stunning display of wealth. Meanwhile, among the villagers on the southern side, a certain Mr Yuan Xian decided to string up his calf-nose shorts. Lest anybody's view be obscured, he made sure to suspend them high in the air, on the end of a bamboo pole. He claimed this was his way of showing enthusiasm for the tradition.

A friend reminded me of a poem composed by the Manchu Dun Cheng, friend of the great novelist Cao Xueqin, which also mentions calf-nose shorts. It was written while Dun was far away and thinking of his friend, who, after a dream-like youth spent in the lap of luxury, found himself subsisting in poverty on the outskirts of Peking. It was during this time that Cao began to write his great novel *The Story of the Stone*.

Having woken from your dream of Yangzhou
You find yourself wearing calf-nose shorts …

If we compare the two, Cao Xueqin the novelist really was much poorer than Sima Xiangru the poet.

My Zhuo Wenjun bear is wearing a typical Han Dynasty wrap-robe (*quju shenyi*). *Quju* refers to the lower hem of her robe, and means it was of the 'extended' variety, long enough to go around the back and be fastened at the waist with a belt. The whole idea of this was to envelop the body completely so as to protect it from exposure. Neither men nor women at the time wore trousers. All they had at that stage were two separate trouser legs.

The accessory in Zhuo Wenjun's hair was called a *buyao*. These developed from the earlier hairpins called *ji* and *zan*. *Buyao* hair accessories were generally woven with gold and silver thread and set in the hair to look like twigs. Pearls and jewels were then suspended from these 'twigs' for adornment. They wobbled around in an attractive fashion. Appearing for the first time in the Warring States period, *buyao* became fashionable some time during the Han Dynasty. They were even exported to the West along the Silk Road. What's interesting about them is that they were not only worn by women, but also by men. They say that Mo Huba, leader of the northern Xianbei nomads, liked them so much that he always insisted on wearing one. 'Buyao' even became his nickname. When translated into the Xianbei language, it sounded more like *murong*, and this eventually was adopted as the official name of the clan. Later these wobbling-twig fashion accessories spread east to Korea and Japan.

Buyao were very popular during the Tang Dynasty. The poet Bai Juyi mentions them in a line of his famous long ballad *The Everlasting Wrong*:

Hair like a cloud, face like a flower,
Headdress which quivered as she walked.[12]

If teddy bears could walk, the accessory in Zhuo Wenjun's hair would wobble and quiver as she walked, too.

---

12 Translated by Herbert Giles, in Minford and Lau eds., *Anthology*, p. 884.

Han Dynasty
(206 BC–AD 220)

Zhang Qian and Hu Mi

Zhang Qian (d.113 BC) was a Minister under Emperor Wu (r.141–87 BC). He is celebrated as the first Chinese who penetrated to the extreme regions of the West; hence he was spoken of by ancient historians as having 'made a road'. About 138 BC he was sent out on a mission to Bactria, but was taken prisoner by the Xiongnu and detained in captivity for over ten years. He managed to escape, and proceeded to Ferghana or Khokand, whence he is said to have brought the walnut and the cultivated grape to China, as well as the art of making wine, which he had learned from the Persians. He is also said to have brought the knotty bamboo and hemp into China. He is considered a national hero for opening China to the world of commercial trade.[13]

There is no specific life of Zhang Qian in the *Records of the Grand Historian*, but Sima Qian did include his story in a collective chapter of biographies. Anybody interested in this envoy who established contact with the Western Regions of China and Central Asia during the Han Dynasty, can read Qi Huan's novel *Pioneering Travels: A Biography of Zhang Qian* (*Zuokong xing: Zhang Qian zhuan*). In this work, the history, characters, setting, and travel paraphernalia have all been carefully detailed.

The word *zuokong* in the novel's title literally means to cut a way through, or to open a road. We have great respect for Zhang Qian because of the message he brought back from his journey: that China should establish contact with its neighbours and trade with them, rather than constantly trying to

13 Based on Giles, *A Chinese Biographical Dictionary*, pp. 12–13.

expand its territory (as was the idea of General Huo Qubing at the time). Zhang also advised against futile searches like that for the mythical Queen Mother of the West and the so-called 'blood-sweating' Ferghana horses (projects supported by the emperor at the time). To his death, Zhang Qian did his utmost to try to persuade Emperor Wu to maintain peaceful co-existence. He was a model diplomat, who knew how to fulfill his mission, but also how to contribute his own ideas. Although Zhang Qian was held captive by the Xiongnu nomads on two occasions and spent thirteen years in exile, he managed to hold fast to his native Han Chinese culture. He continued to do this even after marrying a foreign Xiongnu princess and having children with her.

In the Han Dynasty, wooden staves called *jiezhang* were used to symbolise the emperor and the state. Those carried by Han Dynasty officials were mostly made of bamboo. They measured about eight feet in length, and had a plume of yak tail feathers attached to them, which were red in the early Han Dynasty, and later changed to yellow. Zhang Qian finally brought his Xiongnu princess back to Han territory with him. I've dressed him in a long Han Dynasty robe. These were fairly easy to move about in because the front lapels of the garment didn't need to be tied around the back.

The Xiongnu princess was called Hu Mi and she's dressed in foreign clothes. Both are exotically adorned. Naturally, Zhang Qian always kept his staff with him. If you're thinking Hu Mi's clothes look rather roomy, that was because she was pregnant. She was a Xiongnu princess perpetuating a Han bloodline. Their child, who was given the surname Zhang, was a beautiful mixed baby nurtured by the two different cultures.

Han Dynasty
(206 BC–AD 220)

Sima Qian

Sima Qian (c.145–c.85 BC) is considered the father of Chinese historiography for his monumental work the *Historical Record* (*Shiji*), known as the *Records of the Grand Historian*, which was begun one generation earlier by his father Sima Tan. It is a history of China covering nearly three thousand years, with biographies of eminent figures. Sima Qian fell into disgrace with Emperor Wu for speaking out in defense of a general named Li Ling. He was subjected to the punishment of castration, which the emperor is said to have at once regretted. Sima Qian was subsequently appointed Minister of State, and held the post until his death.[14]

If I had to choose a single book to take to a desert island, it would have to be the *Records of the Grand Historian*. Besides being the most important work of history covering pre-Qin times to the early Han Dynasty, it is extremely well-written, and reads like a brilliant novel, too. The Grand Historian[15] himself invented the biographical style of history. In fact, he was also the pioneer of historical fiction. He wrote the biographies of so many figures from history, but who will write his? None of us know what became of him in his final years, but he must have suffered enormously. His only crime was to express views which differed from those held at court, and for this he was viciously punished. It shows just how terrifying that sort of unrestrained power can be. The disgrace was not so much Sima Qian's, as that

14 Based on Giles, *A Chinese Biographical Dictionary*, pp. 666–667.

15 'The Grand Historian' is the title by which Sima Qian refers to himself in the *Records of the Grand Historian*.

of Emperor Wu, whose ambition knew no bounds. Sima Qian showed no remorse for the entirety of his remaining life. On the contrary, it was the emperor who, in his final years, issued a special decree to take the blame upon himself.

The robe I made for the Grand Historian is called a *chanyu* which is a normal Han Dynasty robe, a *zhiju shenyi*, that doesn't need to be wound around the back. It is casual wear, with a wide, decorative hem along the bottom and the lapels. Those going to court to have an audience with the emperor were required to wear the more formal Han Dynasty robes, *quju shenyi* instead. What is a *quju shenyi*? Well, to begin with, the overlapping lapel at the front of the garment is called the *ren*. If it is done up on the right side, the garment is called a 'right lapel' robe. If it is done up on the left side, it is called a 'left lapel' robe. As Confucius said:

For Guan Zhong, we should wear our hair loose
And fasten our gowns on the left lapel.

In other words, when Han Chinese of the Zhou Dynasty wore these robes, they were done up on the right side. The northern nomads fastened theirs on the left, as had always been the case. Then if another piece of material is joined on to the right side of the lapel, it becomes an 'extended lapel' robe. With a longer lapel, it needed to be wound around the back when dressing. This kind of garment was known as a *quju shenyi*.

The *Records of the Grand Historian* contains an episode in which a nobleman, Marquis Tian of Wu'an, casually wore one of these informal robes (like the one worn by my Grand Historian bear here) to meet the emperor in the palace. This was regarded as such a disrespectful act that he lost his land over it.

In his poem *The Four Sorrows*, when Zhang Heng wrote:

With what can I repay a mink coat given me by a beauty?

With a bright moon pearl …

The 'coat' he was writing about would actually have been one of these robes made from mink pelt. The clothes the Grand Historian wore weren't so precious as that. In fact they were made of simple cotton. He doesn't need to wear a belt, his scented butterfly sachet can just dangle there on its own. Long live the Grand Historian!

Wei, Jin, and Southern and Northern Dynasties (220–589)

Cao Zhi and the Goddess of the Luo

Cao Zhi (192–232) was the third son of the warlord Cao Cao. At ten years of age he already excelled in composition, so much so that his father thought he must be a plagiarist; but he settled the question by producing off-hand poems on any given theme. He was a great favourite of his father, until he made a serious mistake on a campaign against Sun Quan and was condemned to death. 'The Goddess of the Luo' is a rhapsody written by Cao Zhi about a beautiful woman who miraculously appeared to him on the banks of the Luo River.[16]

Cao Zhi's rhapsodic prose-poem *The Goddess of the Luo* and Gu Kaizhi's scroll painting illustrating the scene caused this nymph to go down in history as the most beautiful goddess in Chinese mythology. She is a dainty fairy who moves with tiny steps, in the most attractive clothes of the Wei-Jin period: a short jacket over a long dress with an apron fastened at the waist. The lower hem of the dress features a row of triangular pleats, or 'comet tails' that splay out like a swallow's tail. There are also colourful silk ribbons fluttering out from the bottom of her skirt that ripple like swirling waves.

The Goddess of the Luo River has her hair styled in a 'snake coil'. This kind of chignon is said to have originated with Lady Zhen, queen consort to Cao Pi, who was in a sense the human original of the nymph. After Lady Zhen moved into the Wei Dynasty palace, a green snake would always come and slither around in front of her while she was was completing her

16 For an excellent translation by Burton Watson, see Minford and Lau eds., *Anthology*, pp. 314–318. Based on Giles, *A Chinese Biographical Dictionary*, p. 756.

toilette, coiling itself into a different kind of knot every day. This snake had a soul; it would never have harmed anyone. Lady Zhen found inspiration in this green snake to style her hair in a different kind of chignon every day.

The thing the goddess is holding in her hand is not a feather fan but an elk-tail whisk (*zhuwei*). A *zhu* is a large elk or deer that walks at the front of its herd, with the other deer following its tail, *wei*. As the name suggests, elk tail whisks were made from the tails of these big deer and symbolised strong leadership.

The famous 'fan' held in the hand of the great strategist Zhuge Liang was also an elk-tail whisk and not a feather fan, as is commonly thought. In the Wei-Jin period, people used to issue military orders using these whisks. Witty intellectuals who engaged in the legendary 'pure talk' (*qingtan*) debates also relied on these whisks as props while they were speaking. *A New Account of the Tales of the World* records the story of two famous pure-talkers called Sun Sheng and Yin Hao. While they were famous for their philosophical dialogues, they were really just carrying on a sort of theatrical banter. When words failed them, they would end up throwing their whisks at each other, and the tail fur would land in their opponent's dish.

The goddess is a water nymph, holding an elk-tail whisk in her hand. She can summon the wind and control the rain; she has the wind and river gods under her command.

As for Cao Zhi (otherwise known as the Prince of Chen), who also composed the highly allegorical *Quatrain of Seven Steps*,[17] I've given him a wide, burgundy robe made of pure silk. He also has a jade waist-pendant suspended with a ribbon. In the painting behind them, some of the prince's attendants are holding a parasol, and others are carrying a bolster. He is wearing an official headdress (*yuanyou guan*). His elder brother Cao Pi was the emperor, and as such wore an imperial headdress (*tongtian guan*) instead. The two headdresses had a similar shape but the emperor's had various decorations on it. I made three official headdresses for Cao Zhi. The drooping piece of fabric on his waistband was an essential part of noble adornment during the Wei-Jin period. Women later developed these into aprons. The nymph with a whisk in her hand is finally bidding the poet-prince farewell. Her memory would haunt him ever after.

---

17 There is a story that Cao Pi, jealous of his brother's literary talents, once commanded Cao Zhi to compose a poem in the time it took to walk seven paces. Cao Zhi promptly produced the following:

> *Once, boiling beans while beanstalks fed the flame,*
> *The beans within the pot began to cry.*
> *We sprang together from the self-same root,*
> *So why are you so bent on cooking us?*

Translated by John Frodsham, in Minford and Lau eds., *Anthology*, p. 427.

Xi Kang and Ruan Xian

The Wei, Jin, and Southern and Northern Dynasties was a chaotic period of disunion when northern China was in the hands of non-Chinese leaders and the south was ruled by a succession of weak and short-lived dynasties. The work of poets and artists of this era reflects the unease and anxiety of Chinese society at the time. Many literati tried to escape the atmosphere of corruption and intrigue by moving away to the country, where they would indulge in drinking, music, and poetry. Xi Kang (sometimes romanised as Ji Kang, 223–262) and Ruan Xian are two of a famous group of scholars, writers, and musicians said to have done just this, and were known as the Seven Sages of the Bamboo Grove. They are alleged to have gathered in a bamboo grove near the house of Xi Kang in Shanyang (in present-day Henan Province) where they celebrated the simple, spontaneous things in life. Although Xi Kang married into the imperial family, and received an official appointment, his favourite study remained that of alchemy and forging iron ('to imitate the activity of the Tao, the Great Smith'). He offended one of the powerful family of Sima Zhao, the regent, and was denounced as a dangerous person and a traitor and condemned to death. Three thousand disciples offered themselves in his place, to no avail. He met his fate with fortitude, calmly watching the shadows thrown by the sun and playing upon his zither.[18]

When I was passing a music shop one day, I saw a display of miniature musical instruments in the window. I went in, chose two,

18 Based on Giles, *A Chinese Biographical Dictionary*, pp. 119–120. For portraits of the Seven Sages and anecdotes from *A New Account of Tales of the World*, see Minford and Lau eds., *Anthology*, pp. 445–473.

and then went home to make teddies of the Seven Sages of the Bamboo Grove.

Xi Kang played the seven-stringed zither. The body of the instrument has a wide head, and a narrow tail. Along the side of the finger board are thirteen small white dots, which mark different notes in the scale. The finest quality ones are made of jade, and the best strings are made of silk. When he was faced with imminent execution, Xi Kang played a tune on his zither called the *Guangling san*.[19] 'San' is the name of this type of free melody; and 'Guangling' was the name of a place in the present-day city of Yangzhou. The music tells the tragic tale of vengeance of Nie Zhen, who assassinated Xia Lei, the Prime Minister of the small State of Han during the Warring States period.

During the Wei-Jin period, men of letters dressed unconventionally. They enjoyed taking their clothes off. Men wore skirts just like women and tied up their hair. Xi Kang is wearing a special sort of skirt featuring a shoulder strap. His hair is done up in a top-knot, which I fashioned according to one of the clay brick impressions of the Seven Sages of the Bamboo Grove found near Nanjing. I think the zither in the brick impression is the wrong way around. Perhaps it was deliberately sketched that way when it was being carved so that Xi Kang could sit facing Ruan Ji.[20]

Ruan Xian is playing a plucked string instrument with a long neck. These are normally called 'moon guitars' after the round shape of the body. Since Ruan played one, they are sometimes called *ruan*. It was the precursor of the famous upright, lute-like instrument called the *pipa*. Ruan's moon guitar had twelve frets and he used a bamboo plectrum to pluck the strings.

I had his hair loose, but it hung down over his face. So I just clamped it back with a peg, which looks very postmodern. Like Xi Kang, he's wearing a skirt with a shoulder strap. They are both

---

19 For the *Guangling san*: see *A New Account of the Tales of the World*. Ch. 6, reprinted in Minford and Lau eds., *Anthology*, p. 457.

20 Ruan Ji (210–263), another of the Seven Sages of the Bamboo Grove, was Ruan Xian's uncle. The wife of Shan Tao, another of the Seven Sages, was said to have been impressed by Ruan Ji and Xi Kang's friendship after she spied on them together. It was described as 'stronger than metal and fragrant as orchids'.

wearing a special kind of shawl as an accessory. There are two famous paintings, *Northern Qi Scholars Collating Classic Texts*[21] and *Gentlemen in Retirement*,[22] which feature groups of literati, all wearing skirts with shoulder straps and chiffon shawls extending down beyond the waist. The shawl is draped around the back of Ruan's shoulders, with the ends hanging in front of his chest. There is a pair of silk ribbons which can be used to tie the ends of the shawl together. It really is a very beautiful garment. It's like the silken headdress worn by Zhuge Liang. After all, who's to say headdresses have to be worn on the head?

---

21 By Yan Liben.

22 By Sun Wei, originally called *Picture of the Seven Sages of the Bamboo Grove*. Over the centuries it was damaged and now only four of the seven characters remain: Shan Tao, Wang Rong, Liu Ling, and Ruan Ji.

Wei, Jin, and Southern and Northern Dynasties (220–589)

Wang Xizhi

Wang Xizhi (303–361) was a writer and official of the Jin Dynasty (265–420), known to later ages as the greatest calligrapher in Chinese history. His most famous calligraphic work is the 'Preface to *Poems Composed at Orchid Pavilion*',[23] the original of which has been lost, and survives only in treasured traced copies. In 2010, a small, four-line Tang Dynasty reproduction of one of Wang's calligraphic scrolls on silk was sold in China at an auction for 308 million RMB. He is said to have invented the modern clerical (*li*) script; and his style was described as 'light as floating clouds, vigorous as a startled dragon'. On one occasion he made a copy of the *Tao Te Ching* for a Taoist priest, receiving in return the present of a flock of rare geese. He was the father of seven sons, two of whom rose to distinction. One of his chief delights was to play with his grandchildren, whom he used to carry about and stuff with sweets.[24]

The Grand Commandant Xi Jian once sent an envoy to the home of the Prime Minister, Wang Dao, to choose a son-in-law for him. Wang guided the envoy out to the eastern wing of the mansion to make the selection. As soon as the news spread that someone from the Xi family was coming to choose a son-in-law, the young men in the eastern wing quickly assumed very reserved and dignified airs. All except for one, who stayed just as he was, stretched out on a couch with his belly exposed. He was

23 This is translated by H. C. Chang alongside a picture of a reproduction of a later copy of the calligraphy in Minford and Lau eds., *Anthology*, pp. 479–482.

24 Based on Giles, *A Chinese Biographical Dictionary*, pp. 821–822.

very relaxed, munching away on something, as though the news hadn't reached him. The Xi family ended up choosing this young man, who turned out to be Wang Xizhi. This story is the origin of the saying 'a good son-in-law on the eastern couch'. The incident is very concisely recorded in *A New Account of the Tales of the World*,[25] in the chapter 'On Elegance'. Why was Wang Xizhi lying on the eastern couch with his belly exposed, anyway?

The general explanation is that he had probably been taking the drug known as Five Mineral Powder[26] and was just feeling its effects in the form of a full body fever. The reason people in the Wei-Jin period loved wearing loose, roomy clothes and exposing themselves in a state of undress is more or less because they were tripping on Taoist psychedelic drugs. Five Mineral Powder was extremely toxic, which could be why Wang Xizhi's letters are often preoccupied with bodily ailments.

Why did Grand Commandant Xi choose him? As a matter of fact, his choice reflects the prevailing attitude of the times. Yes, they were particular about family background, but they placed the ability to be oneself above the ability to appear well-mannered. They also considered the ability to tolerate eccentricity to be a sign of good taste and elegance in itself. These sorts of people would have preferred the running style of calligraphy to the more formal script. (The wild cursive script hadn't yet developed.) As for their clothes, they preferred them to be loose and comfortable rather than tight. The fewer garments they wore, the better.

Another celebrated scholar of the Wei-Jin period was Liu Ling, who came before Wang Xizhi. It was he who considered heaven and earth his home, and his house his clothes.[27] If Grand Commandant Xi had encountered Liu Ling before he met Wang Xizhi, which of the two do you think he would have chosen?

My Wang Xizhi, Xi Kang, and Ruan Xian teddies are all made from pure white South American alpaca wool. It's bright, beautiful, and stretchy; normally reserved for making polar bears. My Wang, Xi, and Ruan bears can all sit or stand. The patterns were all specially designed for this purpose. The arms needed to be able to bend. I also had to extend Wang's belly a little so as to have enough to 'expose'. Their outfits are all identical. Wang Xizhi has a large goose behind him, which was a present from my teacher. His pillow was called a 'hidden bag', the equivalent of our modern bolsters. In the Wei-Jin period, people didn't yet have chairs. They would simply sit or kneel around a small table. When sitting with their legs out in front, they would use these bolsters for support. The famous scroll painting already referred to, *Northern Qi Scholars Collating Classic Texts*, features one such bolster being carried by a maid. It looks like a big pillow.

25 A fifth century collection of anecdotes compiled by Liu Yiqing (403–444).

26 Also known as Cold Food Powder. This was a poisonous psychoactive drug popular in the Wei, Jin, and Southern and Northern Dynasties and the later Tang Dynasty, used medicinally and recreationally. People would eat cold food and bathe in cold water to counteract the hyperthermia induced by the drug.

27 In other words, he was a nudist.

Tao Yuanming

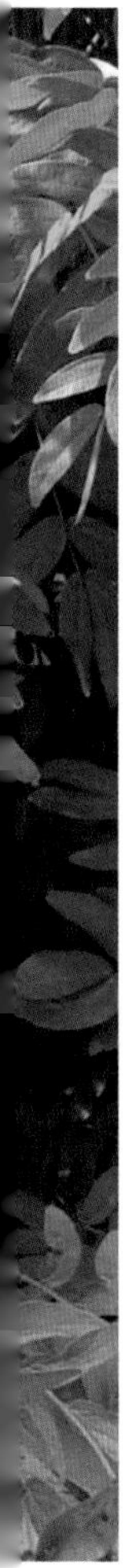

Tao Qian (c.365–427) commonly known as Tao Yuanming, is one of the most widely admired early Chinese poets and foremost of the 'nature' or 'recluse' poets who left society to live in the countryside. He was a youth of wide reading and great ambition, compelled by poverty to become an official underling; but after a few days he resigned and went home, where he made himself ill by overwork in the fields. He was appointed Magistrate at Pengze, Jiangxi, but held the post for only 83 days, objecting to receive a superior officer with the proper ceremony on the ground that he 'could not crook the hinges of his back for five pecks of rice a day', as was the regular pay of a magistrate. Retiring into private life he occupied himself with poetry, music and the culture of flowers, especially chrysanthemums which are inseparably associated with his name. Tao Yuanming wrote a fanciful autobiographical sketch called 'The Gentleman of the Five Willow Trees', written when he was a young man.[28]

I pluck chrysanthemums under the eastern hedge
And gaze afar towards the southern mountains.[29]

In the beginning of his seclusion, Tao Yuanming still had servants and eight or nine thatched cottages. So his clothes should have been quite good. People in the Wei-Jin period liked to

28 Based on Giles, *A Chinese Biographical Dictionary*, pp. 717–718. A translation of his autobiographical sketch by J. R. Hightower can be found in Minford and Lau eds., *Anthology*, pp. 493–495.

29 This quotation is two lines from the third of Tao's *Four Poems Written While Drunk*, translated by William Acker, in Minford and Lau eds., *Anthology*, pp. 503–504.

wear loose-fitting clothes with generous sleeves. For one, the strict Confucian code of behaviour and ethics had relaxed; the literati didn't need to follow any strict rules of etiquette. In addition to this, Taoist psychedelic drugs like Five Mineral Powder[30] which brought on fevers were in vogue. As people often felt hot, they preferred loose, roomy clothes. The fashion of the time was to wear a skirt with a shoulder strap and a length of cloth draped around the shoulders, tied together at the chest with silk ribbons. Tao Yuanming, however, didn't dress like this at all. Some time later, he took a turn for the worse financially. 'The Gentleman of the Five Willow Trees' is really about him, and his day to day life spent in shabby, short clothes in need of mending.

Drinking is mentioned in almost every one of his poems. He suffered from gout, probably caused by excessive consumption of wine and meat. He had difficulty walking and usually needed someone to support, if not carry him. Even standing was problematic if he had to do it for more than a short while. Something that remained unchanged was his love of chrysanthemums, together with his noble character and sterling integrity. Politically speaking, the Wei-Jin era was very dangerous. The philosopher Mou Zongsan (1909–1995) once said that most of the distinguished men of letters of that time died unnatural deaths as a result of one sinister political conspiracy or another. Tao Yuanming survived because he understood the situation only too well. Behind those drunken eyes of his, he saw things very clearly.

When Tao Yuanming 'withdrew from the world', he really did withdraw from the world. He worked the fields himself. All of his friends were country folk.

Meeting each other we do not talk at random,

But only speak of how the hemp and mulberry grow.[31]

'Not talk at random'; what a pointed statement in an era obsessed with obscure deliberations and pretensions! We can almost feel his sense of triumph in the lines.

I think country clothes suit Tao Yuanming best. I fashioned some wide-legged trousers for him, which were in vogue at the time. By this stage trousers had fully developed. He's wearing a wrap-around robe that extends down to his knees. Short, waist-length garments were called *ru*, long, full-length ones were called *pao*, and those that were neither short nor long were called *ao*. He is also wearing a square cloth scarf tied to his head which is actually just a square piece of material. You just tie the two front corners together round the back of the head and the two at the back around the forehead. They later decided to lengthen the four corners, and so many different tying styles emerged. The fashion in the Tang Dynasty was to let the two at the back hang down to look like ribbons suspended from the back of the head. We can discuss the long and convoluted history of head wraps later. Back to Tao Yuanming. One day, he was paid a visit by the Prefectural Magistrate. When the time came to serve the rice wine, the magistrate was surprised to see Tao untie his head cloth and use it to strain the wine. Once he had poured the wine through the cloth, he simply tied it back on to his head.

---

30 See *supra* note in essay on Wang Xizhi.

31 From the second of *Five Poems on Returning to Dwell in the Country*. Translated by William Acker in Minford and Lau eds., *Anthology*, p. 500.

Sui Dynasty (581–618)

The Gallant Trio

In this essay we meet three characters first introduced in the early story 'The Curly-Bearded Hero', attributed by some to the Late Tang Dynasty Taoist writer Du Guangting (850–933). It deals with the period at the end of the Sui Dynasty and the emergence of the man who was to become the founder of the Tang Dynasty, Li Shimin.[32]

Yang Guang (569–618) was second son of Yang Jian, first emperor of the Sui dynasty, whom he is said to have assassinated, as well as his elder brother. Succeeding to the throne in 605, he gave himself up to extravagance and debauchery, spending vast sums over his palace and pleasure-grounds. Yang committed to several large construction projects at frightful sacrifice, including the completion of the Grand Canal, and the construction of another Great Wall. He ordered several expansionist military expeditions, including the invasion of Goguryeo (modern Korea) and Champa (modern Vietnam).[33]

The period at the end of the Sui Dynasty was a turbulent time. The last emperor of the Sui Dynasty, Emperor Yang, had an arrogant and overbearing councillor by the name of Yang Su. One day, a commoner called Li Jing paid a visit to Yang Su. A singsong girl happened to be loitering in the vicinity, holding a red whisk in her hand.

32 See Minford and Lau eds., *Anthology*, pp. 1057–1064.

33 Based on Giles, *A Chinese Biographical Dictionary*, pp. 907–908.

She had eyes for no one but Li Jing. On his way out, Li met the singsong girl under the eaves of the veranda. She asked him where he was staying.

In the middle of the night there came a knock on the door. It turned out to be the same girl, Red Whisk, saying:

The creeper vine cannot live alone,
It needs to climb a tall tree ...

Several months later, she disguised herself as a man and ran away with Li on horseback. On their way, they came across a rather wild-looking vagabond with curly hair about his face. His surname was Zhang. Red Whisk professed herself to be of the same surname, by which means, she and Curly were able to become 'brother and sister'. This resolved any suspicion or jealousy between the two men. Red Whisk had formerly been a singsong girl and had received her name from the whisk she carried around with her. Hers was not a feather duster. She was not a maidservant; she didn't need to do any sweeping or dusting. Her whisk was mostly used for playing with Pekingese dogs.

Women in the Sui and Tang Dynasties did themselves up beautifully. They wore shirts and skirts, but moved the waistband of the skirts up to the chest line, which meant they could dispense with shirts altogether and simply drape a length of chiffon around their shoulders. In addition to that, it was thought attractive to be plump, as is

apparent from the tri-coloured glazed pottery and frescoes of the Tang Dynasty. (But isn't it strange how the 'plumpness' appears mainly on the face, not the body ...). Tang Dynasty women were voluptuous.

When Red Whisk ran away with Li Jing she was wearing a violet dress and a hat. Ordinary gowns in the Tang Dynasty had neither Chinese-style buttons down the front nor slanting lapels; they were worn open. Curly and Li Jing wore round-collared gowns. Round collars had no decorative trimmings, so they would not have stood out while wearing them. Li Jing's long gown is called a 'band robe', because there was a wide band of fabric sewn on horizontally below the knee. Naturally the leather belt had to be fastened, and this was done not with one piece of material, but two. A strip of silk was fastened around the waist to hold the garment in place, at the front to one side, to be precise. Then the belt was worn on the outside and from it ornaments like knives and swords, fish-shaped pouches, and jade pendants were hung. These would dangle about the small of the back.

The culture of the Tang Dynasty was hybrid and multi-cultural. China was 'neither arrogant, nor servile' to the outside world; it was a glorious period of cultural diversity. The alien style dress (or *hufu*) that came in from

Central Asia via the Silk Road became popular and many chose to copy the nomadic herdsmen of the north by wearing leather belts with a series of small holes for hanging things like knives, swords, handkerchiefs, cylindrical needle cases, and knife sharpeners. These items were called the 'seven trappings'. For a time in the early Tang Dynasty, there was a rule which required government officials to wear a Belt of Trappings around their waists. Military officers were required to copy the northern ethnic groups in so far as actually hanging seven odds and ends from their belts. As the nomadic herdsmen had to move around in search of new pastures, they had a real need to carry such things on their person. But for the Chinese living in the Central Plain, they were more like accessories.

Since we're on the subject, interestingly, this kind of adornment was also popular with maids in the imperial palace. They didn't find these knick-knacks to be a hindrance, indeed they even wore them while dancing. Princess Taiping once performed for her parents, Emperor Gaozong and Empress Wu Zetian, with seven such trappings dangling around her waist.

I made a Belt of Seven Trappings for Curly, too. He doesn't have enough whiskers here. At first they were quite long, but I accidently cut them off when I was sewing up his face. I'm so sorry. They should grow back soon.

Tang Dynasty
(618–907)

Xuanzang

Xuanzang (602–664) is the religious designation of a man whose original name was Chen Yi. A native of Henan, he became a Buddhist monk when only 20 years old and in the year 629, reportedly following a dream, set out for India, with a view to visit its holy places and to bring back copies of the sacred books of Buddhism. He returned with six hundred and fifty-seven Buddhist books, besides many images and pictures, and one hundred and fifty relics. He spent the rest of his life translating these books, with the help of several learned monks appointed by the emperor. The manuscript of his *Record of Western Countries* was presented to the emperor in 646. His expedition inspired one of the classic novels of Chinese literature, Wu Cheng'en's *Journey to the West*, written in the Ming Dynasty.[34]

In the last section of the famous scroll painting *Along the River during the Qingming Festival*, there is an itinerant monk among the pedestrians standing in front of a 'four-eyed' well.[35] He can be identified by his rucksack. Later, in the Song Dynasty, rucksacks resembled enormous bamboo racks, which covered not only the length of the wearer's back but extended up beyond the top of the head. These would have been used by many travellers at the time. But earlier in the Tang Dynasty, prior to this, such a large pack might have been a novelty. In the illustration on the front of the novel *Great Tang Record of Western Countries*, Xuanzang is dressed in exactly this kind of

34 Based on Giles, *A Chinese Biographical Dictionary*, p. 313.

35 These ancient wells were a single cavity covered by a stone slab with four holes in it for drawing water.

gear. The rucksacks used by monks in the Song Dynasty were very cumbersome, with several odds and ends swinging from them, rather like a street vendor's shoulder pole. The rucksacks carried by monks during the Tang Dynasty were simply called Racks. They had shelves for books which were filled with Holy Scripture, and an oil lamp that would hang down from the top of the frame.

Since Xuanzang's journey to the West was illegal, he had to travel by night and hide during the day. His oil lamp would have allowed him to read his Scripture and to light his path. Later, explorers and miners would take up this method to venture into underground caves. Xuanzang was the first exchange student to 'venture abroad with a rack full of books', as they say. Besides, for his outfit alone he deserves to go down in history as an amazing travel gear designer. Nevertheless, when the time came for me to make one of these Racks for a teddy bear, I didn't know where to start. I couldn't find any mottled bamboo with the proper speckles on it, and bending and binding bamboo was quite beyond me. I managed to find a wooden shelf and box which I nailed and glued together to pass for a Rack. In the end my teacher helped me to cut and paste some balsa wood and bamboo sticks together. There was a foreigner at my teddy bear exhibition who just stood there staring at Xuanzang. He asked how much he would cost. All I could say was that he was not for sale.

Besides his oil lamp, what else did Xuanzang take with him on his journey? I've given him a walking stick and an umbrella. Since he has to carry his large Rack of books, he needn't wear a full Buddhist cassock. A simple monk's robe will suffice. I think a knee-length one would be good for walking. Naturally he is wearing straw sandals.

When it came to making those, I was baffled again. I ended up knitting them with wool and needles, but they might have been stronger had I used a crochet hook.

In the painting Xuanzang is wearing an earring, so I've given the bear one too. It looks like he's carrying a sword, but it's actually a walking stick. The Xuanzang I've made is not the handsome, delicate, pale-skinned youth the demons and monsters want to eat in *Journey to the West*, but the historical Master Tripitaka from *Great Tang Record of Western Countries*. Having crossed the desert and been completely battered by the wind and blistered by the sun along the way he would have been very tanned indeed. When I was giving him his tonsure, I almost couldn't bear to say goodbye to his hair. Mohair is so beautiful, and of course extremely expensive. Cutting off all that hair was like throwing away a pile of cash. It was really hard to see it go.

Tang Dynasty
(618–907)

Lady Gongsun

The celebrated beauty Lady Gongsun stood unsurpassed as the best dancer in the court of Emperor Xuanzong of Tang. Outside the palace, large crowds would gather for her public performances, which she gave in military costume, wielding a pair of swords. She trained several apprentices, the most successful of whom was Twelfth Lady Li. After the An Lushan Rebellion which began in 755, the performers of her Pear Garden Palace School were scattered, and with them, her legendary martial arts.

Lady Gongsun was an outstanding dancer of the Tang Dynasty. She was an expert in dances featuring swords and felt hats. Not only did she perform in the imperial court, she would often tour and perform for the regular public. The wild cursive script of the famous calligrapher Zhang Xu is said to have been inspired by Lady Gongsun's dancing. The famous poet Du Fu saw her perform when he was a child. Years later he witnessed a performance given by one of her pupils, Twelfth Lady Li, which made him remember the past and record his feelings. His now famous poem, *Ballad on Seeing a Pupil of the Lady Gongsun Dance the Sword Mime*,[36] is an example of the subtle transformation and transmission of ideas that runs through Chinese literature and art.

Dances in the Tang Dynasty fell into two main categories: the 'vigorous', and the 'gentle'. Dancers who wore the feathered Taoist

36 Translated by Arthur Cooper in Minford and Lau eds., *Anthology*, pp. 804–807. Cf. exegesis and translation by David Hawkes in his *A Little Primer of Tu Fu* (The Chinese University of Hong Kong Press and New York Review Books, 2016), pp. 204–216.

immortal robes belonged to the 'gentle' variety, and those wielding swords to the 'vigorous' kind.

Sikong Tu's poem *Sword Dance* has the lines:

In vain the greatest dancer of her day

Trained girls to love military uniforms ...

From the poem we can tell that this was a kind of dance performed by girls in military uniform. It involved bold, vigorous movements set to a rousing rhythm. If a dancer is going to dance with swords, they don't need to be an expert, but they need to know roughly what they're doing. Then even if they can't do the dance properly, they can still do it as a kind of aerobic exercise. For the sake of my health I tried to learn *taijijian*. Of course I was never very good, but now, oh dear, I've just forgotten how to do it altogether.

I stitched together a suit of armour for Lady Gongsun, of the 'double-faced' variety. In other words, it has one plate for the chest and one for the back. The two plates are bound by leather straps over the shoulders. Battle armour was traditionally made of metal plates, mostly iron or copper. The Guard of Honour at the imperial court wore magnificent suits of armour which were padded with cotton and covered in brocade. Dancers also wore cotton-padded armour as a kind of costume.

Lady Gongsun is wearing a strip of cloth as a headband. This was a proper military article in her day. The colour of the band distinguished the soldier's battalion and rank. After the Song Dynasty they became ordinary civilian accessories and stayed in fashion until the Ming Dynasty.

Song Dynasty
(960–1279)

Judge Bao

Bao Zheng (999–1062) was a native of Hefei in Anhui, and a famous judge. In this capacity he gained great popularity by his unswerving integrity, which gave rise to the saying, 'You can't bribe either Pluto or old Bao'. His gravity of demeanour was such that he is said never to have been known to smile. Hence another saying, 'Judge Bao laughs when the Yellow River is clear'—very seldom. The collection of criminal cases published under his name and entitled *Longtu Gong An* is of course a forgery.[37]

Judge Bao lived in the city of Kaifeng, the old capital of the Northern Song Dynasty. He was known as the 'Clear Sky Judge' because he was completely clear of any taint of corruption. He was widely loved and respected for this, as an honourable exception to the countless corrupt officials and miscarriages of justice that have plagued Chinese history. His Three Guillotines, which featured the heads of a dog, tiger, and dragon, were mightily feared. The moment one of the blades was raised, the public felt a thrill of satisfaction that justice was being served. Bao is the main character in a large number of Yuan Dynasty courtroom dramas, such as *The Chalk Circle* and *The Case of the Black Bowl*, which were hugely popular. Judge Bao certainly had his hands full:

> *By day a judge in this world,*
> *By night in the other,*

As they say, insisting he used to work through the night to pass judgement on ghosts and spirits.

37 Based on Giles, *A Chinese Biographical Dictionary*, p. 618.

What did Judge Bao wear? The robes of an official, of course. He was a Grand Secretary in the Dragon-Design Pavilion, after all. All the officials there above the third rank wore deep burgundy robes. The round medallions on his chest and shoulder are embroidered with flowers. From his belt hangs a goldfish pouch. These little pouches were originally designed to show the rank of the wearer. These were later reduced to mere decorative accessories, as was the case with the noble apron worn by Cao Zhi.

Judge Bao was a real person, but I'm afraid the story of the crescent moon birthmark on his forehead comes straight out of a novel called *The Seven Heroes and Five Gallants* and was later made popular in television dramas. I didn't give him a crescent moon on his forehead or a dark face. Once at a bear exhibition of mine, I overheard some people saying, 'How come this Judge Bao doesn't have anything on his forehead?' I didn't take any notice of them. But my teacher came running over, made a big fuss, and immediately started scratching a crescent moon on his forehead with the prong of her belt.

Since Judge Bao is wearing official robes, he needs an official headdress too. He has one. Official headdresses in the Song Dynasty were extremely exaggerated. The side-flaps, or 'wings', extended to left and right, about a foot to each side. Apparently these hats were designed like this to prevent officials at court from getting close enough to whisper in one another's ears. In the eyes of the emperor, officials, no matter how senior, were no more than children.

This being the case, and especially since the head-cloth had developed into the official headdress by this stage, how come Judge Bao isn't wearing one? Here's the story. His headdress was blown off by a big gust of wind and he was just about to go and search for it. As he was setting out to find it, he received an urgent new case to solve. The inside story of that case, which directly implicated the emperor himself, would later form the plot of *The Wild Cat Switched for the Crown Prince*.

(Mongol) Yuan Dynasty
(1260–1368)

Genghis Khan

Genghis Khan (1162–1227) was the famous ruler of the Mongols. Born on the banks of the Onon, his father Yesukai, a Mongol chieftan, named him Temüjin, after a Tartar rival whom he had recently vanquished. Yesukai died when he was only thirteen years old; whereupon various tribes threw off their allegiances. But Temüjin and his mother soon asserted their ascendency. After offering his services to the Jins, who then ruled over the north of China, he conducted successful campaigns against various Tartar tribes; and in 1206 he felt himself powerful enough to assume an imperial title, meaning 'universal ruler', and began arranging his invasion of northern China. In 1209 he captured a pass of the Great Wall and Ningxia in Gansu. By 1214 he was master of all the enemy's territory north of the Yellow River, except Peking. Following his submission of Korea, he turned his attention to Central Asia. By 1221 he ruled Tashkent, Bukhara, Samarkand, and other cities. From this time until his death, his career was one of slaughter and conquest.[38]

Genghis Khan is the national hero of the Mongol people. He united previously disparate tribes, freeing them from the shackles that had bound them since the Jurchen Jin Dynasty. He organised the Mongol herdsmen into groups of ten, one hundred, one thousand, and ten thousand households. He established a head chief for each and formalised the civil and criminal codes into Mongol Common Law. He also appointed an official to take charge of religious affairs and develop a Mongolian script

38 Based on Giles, *A Chinese Biographical Dictionary*, pp. 240–241.

out of the existing Uyghur script. This new script was taught to the younger generation, and from then on the Mongols had their own written language.

Genghis Khan conquered his empire on horseback. He didn't impose Shamanism on his new subjects, but whenever he attacked a city, he ordered the massacre of the Han Chinese population. He was a ruthless conqueror, who obviously had no idea how to govern an empire when not on his horse. Fortunately, he appointed the Khitan Yelu Chucai, who made him realise the importance of rules and regulations in state administration. To build a nation, it is not enough to simply conquer territory; one must win the hearts and minds of the people. Order must be reestablished before a society can become stable. The imperial examination system was reopened and Confucian scholars were selected as officials. Yelu Chucai assisted Genghis Khan and Ogedei to run the state for thirty years. Kublai Khan, the first formal Mongol emperor of China, appointed a Han Chinese called Liu Bingzhong as one of his principal advisers. Liu changed the name of the dynasty to Da Yuan, meaning 'Great Origin', taken from the *Book of Changes*. He built the Mongol capital, which formed the foundation for present-day Peking, in accordance with the *Rites of Zhou*, and established the proper Confucian ritual ceremonies, laying down rules and regulations for the layout and specifications of the imperial city. These remained in practice throughout the later Ming and Qing Dynasties. Those who say the Mongols had no respect for Han Chinese culture are not completely correct.

The outfit I've made for Genghis Khan is a long robe with the jacket and skirt sewn together. The lower garment has wide pleats, like a roomy 'gathered' skirt. The item around his middle is a multi-layered cummerbund. I think it should be sewn with coloured thread and is not complete until it has been wound round the waist thirty times. The history of Chinese clothing cannot disregard the contribution of the Mongols because it was during their dynasty that buttons came into common use for the first time. You can see a row of knotted buttons on his cummerbund. Buttons may be small, but their importance mustn't be underestimated. The slightest change in a button's positioning can change the hang of an entire garment.

At the Stone Age site excavated at Lingjing in Xuchang, Henan, various items related to personal dress and adornment have been discovered, such as buttons fashioned from teeth, needles, and pieces of ochre pigment. Initial findings indicate that people had brilliant red garments fashioned from hide as early as fifteen thousand years ago. The buttons made from teeth are a rare early case. The true introduction of the button had to wait for the Mongols.

Naturally, Genghis Khan is dressed in a fur cape. He has a quiver made from leopard skin on his hip. The standard hairstyle for men at the time was known as 'three nets', for which the head was shaved, except for three clumps of long hair. One protruded over the forehead, and the other two hung down past the shoulders in braids on either side of the head.

Ming Dynasty
(1368–1644)

Zheng He

Zheng He (1371–1433 or 1435), formerly written Cheng Ho, was a Hui Chinese eunuch who served as a fleet admiral, explorer, and diplomat under the Yongle Emperor. He conducted seven sea voyages in massive teak ships, trading and collecting tribute in the Eastern Pacific and Indian Oceans. He arranged for many states to send envoys back with him to China, and later returned with the foreign envoys to their home states in order to open trading relations. After his death, the thirty countries with which he had reopened relations ceased to deal with China. He has been said by some to have introduced opium-smoking into China.[39]

If you were living in the city of Suzhou during the reign of the Yongle Emperor in the fifteenth century, you almost certainly would have gone down to the Liu Family Dock to see Zheng He's fleet embark upon its voyage to the Western Seas.[40] There were probably just as many people there to see the fleet off as the entire crew setting sail. There were sixty-two large ships waiting at the port, with a crew of twenty-eight thousand.[41] Silk standards fluttered on the masts; firecrackers

39 Based on Giles, *A Chinese Biographical Dictionary*, p. 112.

40 Zheng He was also known as Sanbao ('Three Treasures') during his service in the Household of the Prince of Yan, Zhu Di, who would later become the Yongle Emperor. The name is a reference to the Three Jewels (*triratna*) in Buddhism. Of course the 'Western Ocean' or Seas in the present context refers to the Indian Ocean. The expedition departed Suzhou on 11 July 1405.

41 The 1405 expedition, the first of Zheng He's seven voyages, consisted of 27,800 men and a fleet of 62 treasure ships supported by approximately 190 smaller ships.

exploded on the shore. The fleet command devolved into various departments. There were sea captains and soldiers; administrators, general managers, clerks, supply officers, and physicians as well as other operational staff, such as labourers, translators, and meteorologists. Everything had been provided for.

Since the ships were built in Fujian Province, they were called *fuchuan* ships. There were many different types of ships in Zheng He's fleets; including the flagship, battle ships, grain transport ships, supply ships, and hospital ships; all with their own names and numbers. The main flagship was the most beautiful, with four decks. It was over four hundred feet long and eighteen feet wide.[42] The ship's hull drew eleven yards of water. The upper deck supported a beautifully decorated palatial structure, like a floating mansion. The middle deck housed the sleeping quarters and the two lower decks stored tribute articles and gifts. This main ship, also known as the 'treasure ship', had nine masts, twelve sails, rigging, and a winch for the anchor. The cabin which housed the rudder contained a 'needle house' and magnetic compass, as well as such things as star charts and marine maps for navigation. There were sixteen medium-sized defensive cannon on the main deck and eight larger cannon on the lower deck.

The prow of the ship sported a pair of large, round dragon eyes, symbolising the imperial presence. The hull was decorated with a half-moon pattern, the stern with eagle orbs. The ships were covered in auspicious symbols like dragons and phoenixes for good luck. The signal ship had prominent red banners and an array of more than twenty flags for signalling the fleet.

At sea, the fleet resembled a large goose in flight; with protruding head, outstretched wings and prominent tail. The flagship took station in the centre, flanked by escort vessels, with patrol boats scouting ahead. Astern were the warships of the rear guard in a formation like the Chinese character for 'precious' (貴).

To each and every country the fleet visited in Asia they took gifts of silk, porcelain, and tea leaves. They returned with spices, precious gemstones, rhinoceroses, elephants, peacocks, and pearls. Zheng's diplomatic missions promoted cultural and economic exchange. Unfortunately the Ming government would later reinstate the ban on maritime relations with foreign countries. In the end, his grand expeditions came to nothing. No matter how gigantic the cost of such a fleet was, in those days, they were building the complex of stone temples and pavilions upon the slopes of the Wudang Mountains in Hubei. There was an abundance of both manpower and natural resources. If these had been used to establish a navy and develop sea transport, China would

---

42 The author wrote that this ship was over four hundred feet high, probably meaning 'long' instead. Exaggerated descriptions, such as claims the ship was over four hundred feet long are ridiculous but typical of the traditional accounts, such as the record in the official Ming History (*Ming shi*). If these fanciful measurements were somehow accurate, the largest ships in the fleet, the 'treasure ships' described in Chinese chronicles would have been several times larger than any other wooden ship ever recorded in history, far surpassing the late 18th century French gunship *l'Orient*, which was 213.3ft (65.18m) long. The first ships to attain 413.4ft (126m) in length were 19th century steamers with iron hulls. Some scholars argue that it is highly unlikely that Zheng He's ship was 450 feet (137.2m) in length. Xin Yuanyou, professor of shipbuilding engineering at Shanghai Jiaotong University goes so far as to estimate the length at a mere 200–250ft (61.0–76.2m), which would make them smaller than the equine, supply, and troop ships in the fleet. See Church, Sally K., 'Zheng He: An Investigation into the Plausibility of 450-FT Treasure Ships,' *Monumenta Serica*, Vol. LIII (2005): 1–43.

never have been in a position to suffer the disastrous invasion by the Eight Nation Alliance at the end of the nineteenth century.

Zheng He was an imperial envoy, a commander and a palace eunuch, so I made him an official robe of the first rank, with a patch featuring red-crowned cranes. I also gave him a cape to wear on top, which was set as a rule by the Ming Dynasty. The robes of all ranking officials had specific patterns on them. The robes of civilian officials had birds symbolising elegance. Robes of military officers had beasts on them symbolising courage and valour. Officials who received the favour of the emperor were granted robes featuring pythons, flying fish, and fighting bulls.

Perhaps Zheng He should be wearing a flying fish robe. The so-called 'flying fish' actually resembled a water dragon, which would have been too complicated for me to consider embroidering. I couldn't sew one if I tried. This has to be his pre-departure outfit, as he would have looked before he set out on his great voyage. He is bursting with ambition and anticipation. He has a map stowed in his belt and a compass hanging from it.

The flamboyant scale of Zheng He's diplomacy far exceeded that of Zhang Qian of the Han Dynasty. Nevertheless, both would have needed the same fierce determination to face the great unknown.

(Manchu) Qing Dynasty
(1644–1911)

Cao Xueqin

Cao Xueqin (1715–1763) was a poet, painter, and novelist. He wrote China's greatest novel, *The Story of the Stone* (also known as *Dream of the Red Chamber*), which was based on his real life experiences growing up in a wealthy aristocratic household. In China, *Stone* enjoys a unique status, comparable to the plays of Shakespeare in the Anglophone world. Apart from its literary merits, Chinese readers recommend it as the best starting point for any understanding of Chinese psychology, culture, and society. The novel has been translated into many languages. For a complete English translation, see David Hawkes and John Minford, *The Story of the Stone* in five volumes published by Penguin Books (1973–1986).

Whenever I reread Chinese classics like *Water Margin*,[43] *Romance of the Three Kingdoms*,[44] and *Strange Tales from a Chinese Studio*,[45] I am immediately plunged back into the story. But when I read *Dream of the Red Chamber*, I feel more than that. Besides being plunged straight back into the story, I feel the author's images begin to drift around me, on and off the page. Since I'm so fond of *Dream of the Red Chamber*, I like the author's *Guide for Making Kites*, too.

43 One of the 'four masterpieces' of Chinese literature; generally attributed to Shi Nai'an (c.1296–1372). It follows a group of outlaws who fight against the government. See infra bear series 'Heroes from Water Margin' in 'Story Bears' section.

44 A 70% historical, 30% fictional account of the end of the Han Dynasty and the Three Kingdoms period in Chinese history attributed to Luo Guanzhong (c.1330–1400).

45 A large collection of supernatural short stories written by Pu Songling (1640–1715).

Novels and short stories are just pages of text, but this book about kites is a feast for the eyes. It is filled with gorgeous colour illustrations. The section on swallows alone features patterns for plump swallows, slim swallows, and swallows flying wing to wing. Then there are patterns for completely different kites, like that for making a goshawk, Luo River goddess, goldfish, or wild goose.

Cao Xueqin's original intention in writing a book about kite-making was as a means to help his poverty-stricken and physically disabled friends. He too was very poor and struggling to make ends meet. He thought, instead of giving money, it would better to give a skill by which one could make one's own living. He also taught the blind how to weave so that they could support themselves.

Throughout the ages of Chinese history, there have been countless writers and poets. Yet how many do we know of who had the generosity to put their own interests aside to offer assistance to those in need by teaching them a skill? Too many have gone on thinking that to part with their knowledge would harm their own interests. Moreover, Cao did this under extremely straitened circumstances. *Dream of the Red Chamber* breaks my heart when I read it, not because of what happens in the story, but because of my sympathy for author. After his family was ruined,[46] Cao lived the rest of his life in dire poverty. He survived on rice gruel and bought wine on credit. On the Mid-Autumn Festival of the twenty eighth year of the Qianlong Emperor's reign (1763), his only son died of illness. Overcome with sadness, Cao would often visit his son's grave and weep bitterly upon it. He began to drink more heavily than ever and soon fell ill himself. He passed away a few months after his son's death on the eve of the Chinese New Year (12 February 1764).[47]

Research into the Cao family maintains that he used to wear a blue cotton gown in his later years. This was called an *erdalian* in Peking dialect. It was a traditional collarless blue cloth gown for men. Early in the Manchu Dynasty, students and scholars were fond of these comfy collarless gowns. In a portrait passed down through the ages, the Manchu poet Nalan Xingde is dressed in one. I was unable to design a specific *erdalian* pattern, so I just made a plain collarless gown out of marine blue cloth for my Cao Xueqin bear. Of course his hair is styled in the form of a long queue. It's not much. Just my small tribute to the greatest master of our profession.

---

46 This episode is reflected in chapter 105 of the novel.

47 Evidence suggests it was in fact 1763. See David Hawkes, *The Story of the Stone*, Vol I: The Golden Days, Introduction, p. 22.

The Empress' New Clothes

This bear is just looking at her outfit, she hasn't put it on yet. She was the model for my series 'Chinese Bears in Antique Garb', and I designed her especially for it. In order to fit into clothes, a bear must keep a fairly slim figure. The head and snout part is long and narrow. Female snouts have to be slightly narrower than male snouts, which are quite wide. Bears have ears which are raised and point backwards. In my attempts to make a bear who could stand steadily, I tried making the arms long and straight without paws and setting the legs very low. I made the soles of the feet flat and wide, and lined them with thick cardboard. I filled the bears with glass beads for extra weight. It took me three years to make a bear who could stand without falling over.

A bear's trunk has five joints, which allow the head, torso, and four limbs to rotate 360 degrees. This is a distinctive feature of the handmade 'art bears' which sets them apart from the regular teddies sold in the shops.

My bears are stuffed with synthetic padding. The head must be as hard as a tennis ball, which took a huge effort for me to achieve. First, the bear's belly is half-filled with plastic pellets to make them look tubby and slightly pot-bellied. Then the rest is stuffed with cotton padding. After that the bear can stand like a model and I can start putting the outfit together. A handsome bear will look beautiful and graceful without any clothes, in fact. All the high-end bears are naked.

Story Bears

Hua Mulan

(from the *Ballad of Mulan*)

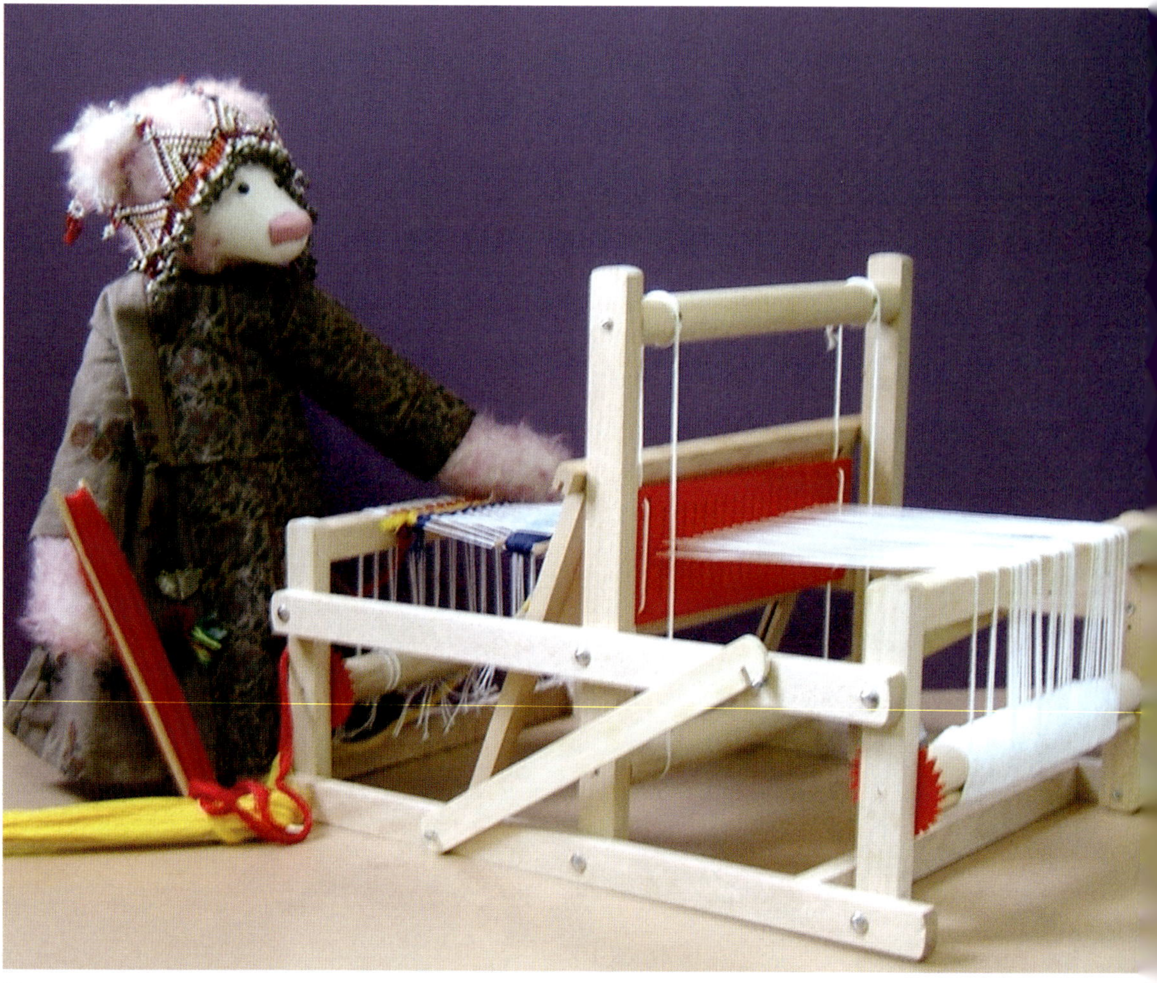

'Click-clack!'

'Wishing to borrow a camel for a thousand miles'

'Putting on makeup in front of the mirror'

'Armour in moonlight'

Heroes from *Water Margin*

Another of the four great novels of Chinese literature,[48] *Water Margin* (also called *Outlaws of the Marsh*) is generally attributed to Shi Nai'an (c.1296–1372). It follows a group of 108 outlaws who gather at a place called Liangshan Marsh (or sometimes Mount Liang), form a large militia and fight against the government. *Water Margin* was based on the exploits of the real outlaw Song Jiang and his companions. The group was active in the Huainan region and surrendered to the Song Dynasty government in 1121.

48 The other three masterpieces being *Romance of the Three Kingdoms*, *Journey to the West*, and *The Story of the Stone*.

Yan Qing

The 'Prodigal Wanderer'

When I first started making bears, the one I most wanted to make was the 'Prodigal Wanderer', Yan Qing. Perhaps it was because I'd written about him in my rather ordinary sequel to the masterpiece *Water Margin*. He's the only character in the novel who wanders freely in the great sea of life, immune to the temptations of fame and fortune. Actually, perhaps the reason I decided to make him was so I could embroider flower tattoos all over his body. I first started him with a piece of beautiful brocade, but it was too thick for me to sew and didn't work. I completely wasted that gorgeous material; it had been woven with gold thread! A Yan Qing bear without any tattoos simply wouldn't look right, so in the end I did manage to put something together for him.

Shi Jin

The 'Nine Tattooed Dragons'

Shi Jin has nine dragons tattooed on his body. Compared to the exquisite illustration of Shi Jin in Chen Hongshou's album *Leaves from Water Margin*, my design is reminiscent of oracle bone inscriptions, it's so clumsy! But because he was the first bear I made for my *Water Margin* series, I treasure him dearly all the same. I gave my bears from *Water Margin* short white fur because it's fairly easy to embroider upon. It would be much more difficult to do embroidery on long fur. There are other advantages to using white fur, like being able to put eye shadow around the eyes and in the ears, which can make the bear seem more three-dimensional. Shi Jin carries a staff, but when it comes to proper martial arts, let's just say if his friends were in need they wouldn't be calling him in first. I'm afraid his skills are all show but no go and he'd be completely useless in a real fight.

Yang Zhi

The 'Blue Faced Beast'

The birthmark on Yang Zhi's face earned him the nickname the 'Blue Faced Beast'. Besides the birthmark, he has some words tattooed on his face, too. The whole thing should read 'EXILED TO DAMING PREFECTURE PEKING FOR MILITARY SERVICE'. I had to leave several characters out because his face is so small. I split what I could fit into three lines of embroidery. He's wearing a sword. It's a pity that I couldn't find anything special enough to be his 'precious sabre' heirloom. Just imagine he's already pawned it while wandering as a destitute outlaw in the badlands of River and Lake.

Shi Qian

The 'Chicken Thief'

The *Water Margin* character Shi Qian is nothing more than a chicken thief. He is certainly not some great treacherous villain. He simply has good sight and hearing. The chicken feather on his head exposes him for what he is. He is carrying a colourful, speckled chicken and has a knife stowed down the side of his leg.

Oh dear, it's wrong, it was supposed to be a rooster.

Zhang Qing

The 'Featherless Arrow'

Zhang Qing, the 'Featherless Arrow', plays a supporting role in the heroes from *Water Margin* series. I have him appear mainly to stand guard with two special weapons. One is a shield with a tiger's head in the middle of it, made from a pair of children's shoes, surrounded by colourful hand-painted patterns. The back of the shield has a rubber ring which can be looped over the arm, too. The other weapon is a tasselled spear with a silver tip. If his martial arts are not up to scratch, this should at least make him *look* brave.

Of silver spear the leaden counterfeit!

He has a bag of pebbles hanging from his belt, and these are his real weapons.

Fancy Dress Ball

Beauty and the Beast

Time is Beauty's worst enemy. But in the world of handicrafts, beauty can break through the prison of time. No matter how much toys deteriorate, they always stay forever young. Teddy bears with black fur are rare. The most famous one was the black teddy made to commemorate the sinking of the Titanic. Black teddies are hard to come by because black thread is so difficult to work with. After more than ten attempts at my 'Beast' bear, I was starting to feel very confident. But then I got his torso upside-down and sewed the buttocks onto his shoulders. I didn't correct it, but left it as an example. I used an animal-print scarf to cover up my mistake. If I hadn't pointed it out I don't think anybody would have noticed.

I really love this bear, he's like a spoiled child. He is holding a white flower in his paws. His eyes are gold and black, and there is a tear drop on his cheek. His top layer of fur is black, but the under layer is brown. I didn't do a motley two-tone bear; my design failed.

Lawrence of Arabia and His Middle Eastern Wife

When I was travelling in Egypt, I bought a *kufiya*. It is a square piece of red and white checkered cloth with a black and gold *igal* for fastening. It was because I found this headdress that I decided to make my Lawrence bear. The Englishman T. E. Lawrence and French writer Pierre Loti were both great lovers of Arab culture. They would never have dismissed Arabs as part of some 'axis of evil', or anything like that. Lawrence is made of black and white two-tone wool, which you can see on his face. His accessory is a miniature silver trumpet. After three years, the silver has tarnished, but I think it suits his tassels even better now.

His Middle Eastern wife has only her eyes exposed. The black cloth she is wearing I bought in Iran where I wore it as a headscarf for a week.

Julius Caesar and the Queen of Egypt

Styled in ancient Egyptian fashion, Cleopatra has a large Eye of Horus sewn upon her face. So she looks best viewed in profile, the special aspect of Egyptian art. She is made from white mohair with shiny gold tips. I still owe her two sceptres.[49] I'll make them for her when I have time.

Caesar is wearing an attractive laurel wreath on his head and striking a stately pose. He has his right hand and foot raised as though issuing an order, with his toga hanging down over his other arm. I chose a beautiful length of silk for him to wear. It is printed with pictures of the opera house in Milan.

49 Cleopatra's sceptre was in the form of a cross.

Belly Dancer

Of course, this girl is doing a belly dance. But in this case, it's a 'beary' dance, too. She's made from a superior, pure white alpaca fleece which is the best for making polar bears. She's wearing a turquoise blue costume, the same colour as her eyes. She chose all her accessories herself when I took her to the jewellery shop.

Princess Iron Fan and the Bull Demon King

Princess Iron Fan and the Bull Demon King are a married couple in the novel *Journey to the West.* The princess is a beautiful demoness living in an underground cave awaiting her husband's return. She refuses to lend the Monkey King her banana-leaf fan to subdue a volcanic mountain range the pilgrims meet. Their encounter was adapted for the first Chinese animated film, *Princess Iron Fan* (1941).

I decided to make Princess Iron Fan after I came across a palm leaf fan in a shop selling folk trinkets. Her clothes are made from Indian mirror-inlay fabric. Both her necklace and large fish pendant earring are pure silver. She hasn't got her fan out at the moment, it's just hanging there. She looks very gentle and calm.

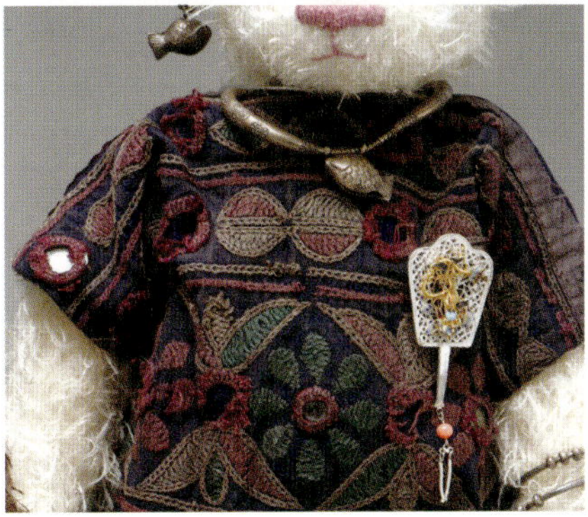

The Bull Demon King has a fluffy coat of coffee-coloured mohair with gold highlights. I thought for a long time about how to make his horns. Eventually I decided to use iron hooks covered in clay. Then I just sewed them on to the crown of his head. I took him to the jewellery shop too to choose his breast plate. I wanted him to look really fierce and powerful, like a Viking. He has earrings, and his feet actually have anklets on them. He's quite avant-garde, isn't he?

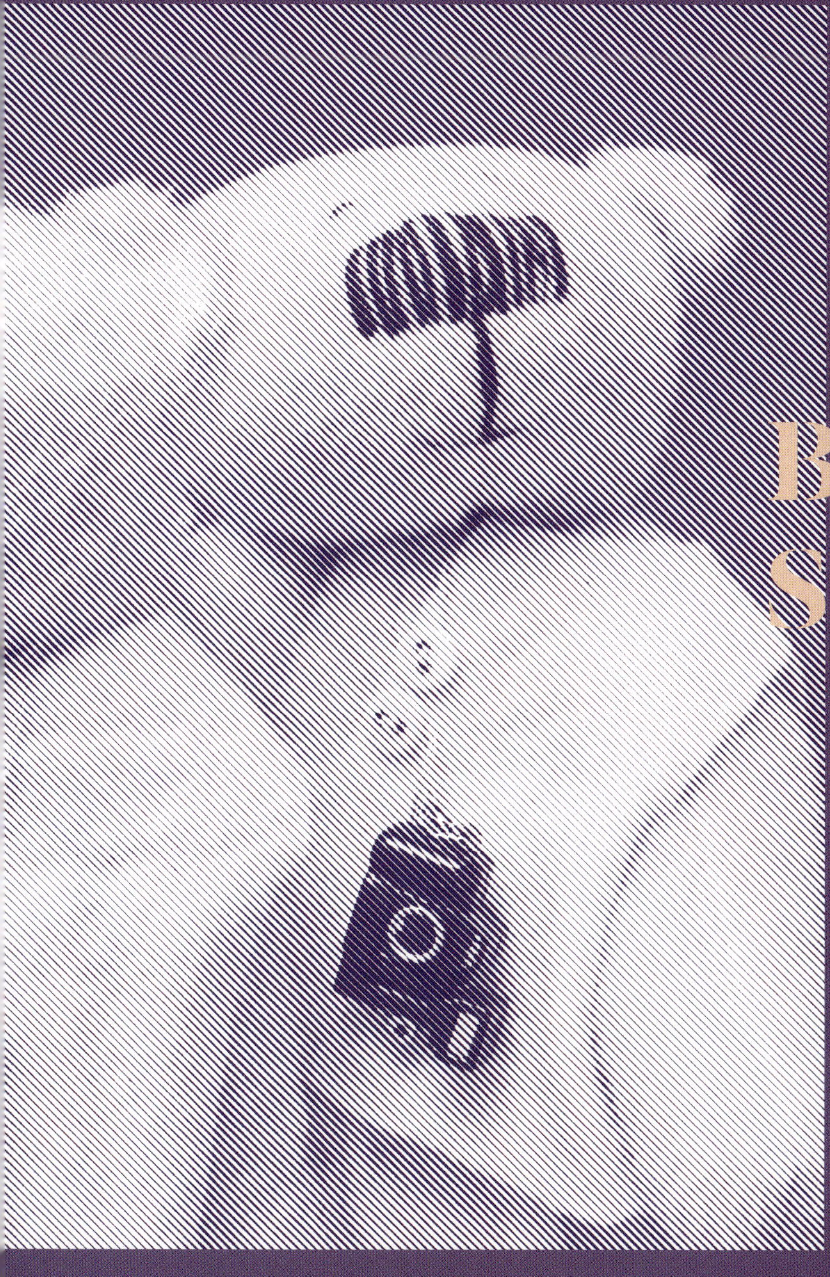

Bear Stories

Clan of the Zebra Noses

Doing housework

Smiling

Brother and sister

Story time with uncle

Looking at a house

Recital

Stealing honey

Acrobats

These acrobat bears are all young males. They're only eighteen centimetres tall. Their fur is fluffy, and they look very cheeky. They have wide noses and are cross-eyed. The troupe is performing Chinese acrobatics. One is doing plate spinning, one is balancing a table, one is doing jar juggling, one is playing with a diabolo.

Busking

Plate spinning

Foot juggling

Jar juggling

Diabolo

The Scarf Faction

What should we do?

Give flowers

You give flowers too

Play marbles

Play pinball

Play dumb

Play blocks

Climb a ladder

Do a jigsaw puzzle

Put on a play

Do the lion dance

The Long Necked Ladies with the Big Eyed Bears

A Long Necked Lady with Snow White's Seven Dwarves

The Long Necked Ladies

We're the long necked ladies
Born big, born tall
Call us weird
We won't mind a bit
A long neck can wear all kinds of necklaces
Ten, twenty, as many as we like
We digest our meals nice and slow
No need for four stomachs
Eve in the Garden of Eden
Picked fruit from the Tree of Knowledge
Thanks to her long neck
Only after she'd eaten it
Did she gain Self-Knowledge
And Modigliani the painter
Found beauty in our long necks
He loved us most of all
We love him too
Count Dracula of course would agree
For whom the one and only measure of beauty
Was … neck length
He lived forever, what a true horror that was—
To remain unchanged for a thousand years!
We're submarines on the horizon
We're periscopes in the crowd
We'd never call other animals ugly
Or consider ourselves unattractive
We are what we are
Ourselves

A Long Necked Lady with Sock Puppet

The Big Eyed Bears

Sailing boat

Watering the flowers

Musical chairs

Injured Moon Bear

China has panda bears, and black bears, too. Pandas are seen as a national treasure, but what about black bears? Another name for the Asian black bear is 'moon bear' because they have a white, V-shaped patch of fur on their chests like a crescent moon. For a long time, black bears have suffered horrendous cruelty. Many have been locked up in narrow cages, in which it is impossible to stand, move, or turn around. Locked in iron 'vests', they have tubes inserted into their gallbladders, and bile extracted on a daily basis. They can barely survive and yet they are unable to die, either. This dreadful business was first seen in North Korea in the early 1960s. Then it spread to mainland China. In recent years an organisation called Moon Bear Rescue has been formed.

Caring for Injured Moon Bear

Bear Friends

Eating rice

Waiting for floating ice

Still waiting

Embroidering

Knitting

Floral bear

Bear with claws

Teddies on Tour

(excerpt)

On the Eurostar

I.

To make my first teddy bear, I used yellow mohair, a type of wool that comes from the fleece of the Angora goat. It is light enough to carry around with me and take when I go travelling. In Holland, I saw some very fine, miniature porcelain clogs. I bought a pair and slung them over my little bear's arm. He flew with me, so I found some feathers for him, and named him 'Yellow Flying Bear'. And thus my bear-making life began. When I was rummaging through a pile of teddy bear books one day, I thought to myself, besides pandas, how come there aren't any Chinese teddy bears?

I decided to make the *Water Margin* series.

There are five bears in the Heroes from *Water Margin*. None of the young people in my class know who they are; they haven't read *Water Margin*, which is no surprise. As a matter of fact many adults know nothing about Shi Jin's tattoos—now this astounds me. I really don't know how to explain the characters on Yang Zhi's face, or the flower behind Yan Qing's ear.

2.

Now you bears are always complaining about how unfair it is that only Yellow Flying Bear comes travelling with me, while the rest of you have to stay behind. The truth is, in recent years my health has taken

Xi Xi with Shi Qian

a turn for the worse and long-distance flights have become hard. I hardly travel at all. I know you must be disappointed. But I have some great news. I've heard about a German man called Mr Boehm who is setting up tours for teddy bears. He's the guide, and takes bears on tours around Germany. I have already signed you all up, you can finally go travelling. I don't mean to nag, but I need to give you a few words of advice before you set out. As you all know, Yellow Flying Bear may seem like a bore in the eyes of other bears, but he's always been very well-behaved. In fact, the others always used to play tricks on him in class. Everyone knew how honest he was. That's why I thought he would be a safe bet to take with me.

You lot, however, are a bunch of rowdy bandits. You would probably cause me endless trouble. How could ever I relax on holidays with you? There will, of course, be some other teddy bears on your tour. Please be nice to them.

When you go through Immigration, ask the officer to stamp your passport. That makes a good souvenir. German immigration officers will always be happy to do this for you. After all, Germany is the home of the teddy bear.

Yan Qing, you can take your flute because it's a musical instrument. Pack it in your cabin luggage. Germans love music, so why not give a little performance in your free time in one of the public squares? You might even end up making enough to buy some sweets. Since you're travelling, why not sample some different cuisine? Don't just go for rice, noodles, and dumplings every time. Let your bellies 'expand their horizons', too. Absorb some culture.

I've tried to teach you table manners. Let me remind you that having soup over there is not like slurping down a noodle soup here at home. Do it quietly, don't draw attention to yourself. When it comes to bread, don't just hold it in your paws and chomp into it. Tear it up into nice little chunks and eat them one by one.

The tour guide will take you into some famous beer halls while you're over there. These are very lively establishments and they're normally full to capacity, with hundreds of people packed inside. There will be folk music playing, and people talking and laughing to their heart's content. It'll be just like your bandit get-togethers on Mount Liang. You can drink as much beer as you like, and even put on a little show. Just don't go making any trouble or getting into any brawls.

Every time you go out, make sure to be neatly and appropriately dressed, especially you, Shi Jin. Don't go around baring your belly to the world. Those dragon tattoos of yours may very well be misinterpreted by the Europeans.

No matter where you are, always keep calm and quiet. Don't squat down at the bus stop, by the roadside, or in shop doorways, like an army of frogs. How unsightly. Don't spit all over the place, either.

Shi Jin, you keep an eye on Shi Qian for me. Don't let him go stealing chickens and catching bird flu. I won't be there to save you. Don't use the flash when taking photographs in the museums. Zhang Qing, don't you go throwing pebbles. You're lucky it's Germany you're going to and not Palestine, or you'd probably get shot.

You all have digital cameras, so bring some photos back, please. You can email some of them to me while you're still over there if you like. That's all, have a great trip!

Yellow Flying Bear

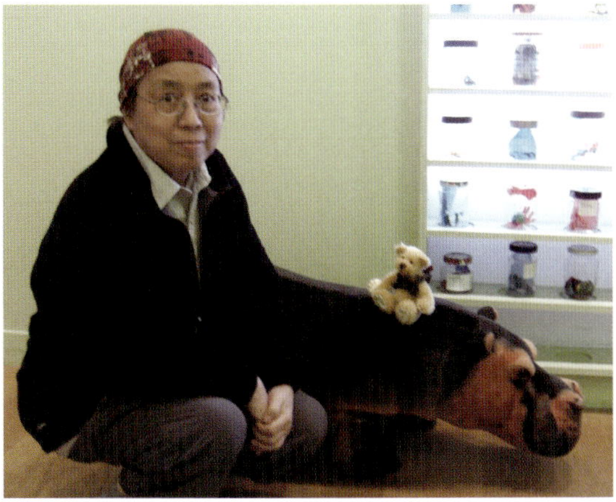

Riding a cow

Flannel Bear with Yellow Flying Bear

Hmm, what looks good?

Sitting in a famous chair

In Utrecht

In Amsterdam

In The Hague

Collectors' Bears

If you want to give a teddy to a child as a gift, why not just buy one of the factory-made ones sold in the shops? They look cute, they're soft, cuddly, and machine washable. If they come wearing clothes, those can be changed. Safety has to come first. Factory teddy bears' eyes are not sewn on with thread; they are punched in like studs. They are firmly set so children can't pull them out and put them in their mouths. Collectors' bears, on the other hand, are unsuitable for children. They're not cheap, and they're not machine washable. That said, each and every one is unique by virtue of being handmade. If you're looking for art teddy bears, very few can be found in Hong Kong. You really have to go to the European and American fairs. They may be found for sale behind the counters of some toy shops.

Germany, America, Switzerland, and even the Netherlands and Japan now have teddy bear trade shows every year, held in big hotels, factories, and ancient castles. Any bear artist can participate if they sign up in advance and hire a stall. The stalls are about the size of an eight-person dining table but cost several hundred euros to hire. The fairs normally only go for two days. Everyone puts their work out on display and for sale. They're lively occasions, with lots of teddy bear fans gathered together in one place. You can find your favourites, meet the makers and have a chat. It's like a fans' teddy bear picnic! The price of a bear can be anything from a few hundred to more than a thousand euros, depending on the size, the quality of the wool, and the reputation of the artist. Bear fairs also hold competitions to encourage new talent. Teddy Bear Total in Germany is the most exciting one because it attracts the most artists. It's always held in the last weekend of April.

I've collected very few bears myself, less than ten. I don't collect mass-produced factory bears, even if they're from a famous manufacturer. I leaf through magazines and ask my friends to look online for me, then I go to Europe to find handmade pieces by bear artists I really like. That said, there are very few bear artists I really like, less than five. Only a small number of artists are truly creative (like Nicole Marschollek) and they seldom exhibit. People always find Nicole's work amazing. I only know of one specialist shop in Munich that sells her bears. Unfortunately my health doesn't allow me to travel long distances to go collecting anymore. My favourite artist of all is Marie Robischon, who lives in Germany. Her bears have a strength and dignity about them, and an awe-inspiring, heroic aura. Every outfit she makes appears to be randomly thrown together, but they always look comfortable and stylish. I once made a special trip to the annual bear fair in Zurich to meet Marie. Like a regular fan would be, I was really excited to meet her, and asked things like, what did she use to fill her bears' bellies? Sand, she said. What kind of sand? Sea sand,

Marie Robischon's bears

Robischon's bears in Chinese dress

or river sand? How do you clean it? And so on; and so forth. These are all trade secrets of the artist, which you may never be able to ask again. I bought two of Marie's bears, which cost me the royalties from two of my books. To me, they're worth it. She knew I had come a long way and she wished me a safe trip home. Every Christmas I go into the children's wear section and buy two new sets of clothes for my Marie bears to wear. I dress them up, take a photo, and email it to Marie. In last year's photo, they were in padded jackets and tiger shoes. I also bought some work by the famous German bear artist Doris Minuth. Her bears look strong and sturdy. They stand firmly on both legs, very calm and steady. You need a lot of strength in your hands to make bears like that.

With Marie Robischon

With Doris Minuth

Memorial Bear

(for my little sister)

Q&A: On Teddies and Traditional Chinese Fashion

Xi Xi in conversation with Ho Fuk-yan (excerpt)

Ho: When did you start making teddy bears?

Xi: In April of 2005. I'd just finished making a doll's house and didn't have room for another one at my place. My right hand was losing more feeling every day; I needed to find some sort of exercise for it. I started learning how to make miniature clay flowers, but eventually found I wasn't that interested in them; and the work was too finicky anyway. My hands and eyes weren't up to making them, so I decided to learn how to make teddy bears instead. At first I was teaching myself, thinking I could DIY as I had done with the doll's houses. I bought a book. It said I'd be able to finish one bear in two hours. It came with a pattern which you could follow, step by step. But mine didn't turn out like a bear at all. It looked like a rat! I wasn't getting anywhere. So I decided to learn properly, with a teacher. No more hodgepodge, no more using buttons for joints ... One day I noticed some reddish-purple mohair on display in a shop down the street. It was gorgeous, and I thought teddies made from that would turn out very nicely. The owner asked me whether I knew how to make teddies. I said I didn't. She said, instead of going ahead with it now on your own, wasting good material and hundreds of dollars, you'd be better off learning how to do it properly first. I can teach you. Wonderful! I replied. Without you teaching me, I'd make a terrible mess. You see, I have some nerve damage in my right hand. And so I became one of her bear-making students. Her name is Gloria, she is the president of the Hong Kong Teddy Bear Association. Noting my age, my thinning grey hair and plain clothes, she only charged me half of the fees. After joining the HKTBA, I got a discount on mohair, too.

Ho: So it was really by chance.

Xi: It took me just over six months to go from beginner to advanced. I was probably the oldest apprentice in the class. Some of my classmates at the time were primary and high school students. And they were all girls.

Ho: These days parents run around taking their children to piano and violin lessons, dancing, extra tuition ... I'd have thought there should be a place where children can go to learn how to make teddy bears and soft toys? And of course it shouldn't be for girls only. There should be more such options for extra-curricular activities. Children could learn traditional opera, or taichi.

Xi: Perhaps. But I've found Hong Kong people have something against teddies. There are three words this Financial Centre is not fond of seeing in a row: Teddy bear market.

Ho: This so-called 'Financial Centre' of Hong Kong is just a big casino.

Xi: Half a year is the time I've spent actually going to classes. I've got quite a bit of free time, and I'm quite into it at the moment. I called my first teddy Yellow Flying Bear because he's yellow, and his fur is so fine. I took him on the plane with me. We went to Holland, Germany, and England. We visited a museum that had a collection of doll's houses and a teddy bear exhibition. After that I went on to make another one, a rather large bear.

A few months after I had started, I discovered that my teacher's teddy bear association holds a competition every year, and students are encouraged to participate. She wanted me to take part. So I designed a teddy bear of Shi Jin from the classic novel *Water Margin*. I chose him so I could do some embroidery of his special 'Nine Dragons Tattoo', which is famous in China. My favourite lines from *Water Margin* are,

Martial arts of flowery play

In real battles do not pay ...

My teacher liked the bears as soon as she saw them. She really encouraged me, saying they were creative. For my next series I made a few more bears who became my *Water Margin* guys: Yan Qing, Shi Qian, Yang Zhi, and Zhang Qing. In technical terms, my young classmates with their nimble fingers and good eyes were far beyond me. They go ahead making all of these figures from the *Holy Bible*, but don't even know the characters from *Water Margin*. They haven't read *Water Margin*.

The times have indeed changed. But learning to make teddies can eventually become a skill. One of my classmates from Shanghai, Esther, opened a restaurant there in Tianzifang. It has a beautiful, quirky teddy bear shop downstairs. She has a collection on display in there. At the very least it's the first kind of teddy bear gallery in mainland China. She teaches bear-making as well.

I tend to make teddies and read at the same time. I've always been a bit of a bookworm, and I like books and magazines about teddies, too. They have all these stories about people embroidering flowers on to their bears. That's what gave me the idea to make Yan Qing from *Water Margin*.

At first I completely failed because I was trying to do it with brocade, which is too firm a fabric for bear-making. You just can't manoeuvre it. I based the Nine Dragons Tattoo on some paintings by Chen Hongshou I remembered. The competition prize was sponsored by a German who just so happened to be the boss of a mohair company. My entry was given a very high mark by the English judge, but the mohair executive thought it didn't deserve the prize. Reason being: I hadn't used mohair produced in his factory. I really don't know anything about mohair brands. Since I needed to embroider flowers on, the only mohair I could have used was the 'short-haired' variety. What would getting the prize have meant to me anyway? My teacher stood up for me and said the use of certain brands of mohair was not a prerequisite.

Making teddy bears is just like making clothes. First you need to draw up a pattern, then cut the fabric. Long-haired mohair and short-haired mohair produce different effects. Trimming the fur on the nose 'thick' or 'thin' will also produce different looks. I used the same pattern for Yellow Flying Bear and the Acrobats, but they turned out to be totally different because I adjusted the length of the paws and feet, the size of the eyes, and the distance between and position of the ears. Ha! So it's true that the body, paws and feet can all grow, but the eyes can't! Upright ears will make the bear seem more alert, drop ears will make the bear look more docile. They'll look different again depending on the way you set the head.

In the end I think it's the ears rather than the eyes that determine the bear's final appearance.

Ho: You don't have to use mohair, do you?

Xi: Not necessarily, any material will do. But if you do use mohair, it won't lose shape or fall apart. Because it's such a tight weave, there's very little give. You can cram the head full of cotton till it's bulging and it won't burst. The outer shell of mohair comes from the fleece of the Angora goat, and the inner-rung is what in English you'd call cotton, which is just a cotton-weave fibre. It comes in every colour imaginable; if you choose a yarn with at least two colours, you can have a different colour at the tip. Your bear will actually be multi-coloured. They turn out beautifully, like a gorgeous patterned rug. Besides all the colours available, mohair comes in 'short' and 'long'-haired varieties. Other materials will crumple and lose their shape, but mohair won't.

Ho: Would you mind saying something about the history of teddy bears?

Xi: 'Teddy bear' is the general name, which came from the nickname of a former American President, Theodore 'Teddy' Roosevelt. But there are different versions of the story about the origin of these toy bears. The Germans and the Americans have their own ways of putting it. The earliest toy bear appeared at the end of the nineteenth century in Germany. It was wooden, had four paws set on four wheels and could be dragged around. Children must have really liked it. In 1893 the Steiff company was founded and began producing toy bears. Steiff have always been the most famous manufacturers, and historically, they are the oldest company. They have constantly been doing research to improve their products and their brand has become really famous. Their success is attributed to their founder, Miss Margarete Steiff. She possessed amazing sewing skills, despite having been in a wheelchair since childhood and having mobility in her right hand only. She was determined as well as extremely imaginative. The first thing she made was a pin cushion in the shape of an elephant, which became a very popular giveaway gift at their family tailor's shop. She then founded the company with her family and made other sorts of toys. Around the turn of the century, just when Steiff were entering the American market, a toy bear once attracted the delight of the guests of honour at a Roosevelt dinner party. Someone asked the bear's name. As it didn't have one, they just took the President's nickname and came up with 'Teddy bear'. Another version links it to one of Roosevelt's hunting trips. They say Roosevelt once let a young injured bear go, and decided to ban bear hunting from then on. Some business people were inspired by the story and secured a registered trademark on 'teddy bear'. However it came about, it definitely had something to do with Roosevelt. Why bother going into it anyway? Teddy bear artists didn't start to appear in large numbers until the 1970s. The main clientele changed from children, who like them as toys, to adults, who like to collect them.

Ho: Did the inspiration for your Chinese Bears in Antique Garb series come from your Heroes from *Water Margin*?

Xi: After that I made the foreign bears for the Fancy Dress Ball, then the Acrobats, and since then I've kept going learning how to make all sorts of bears. I've put music boxes in their bellies, added claws, and worked out how to move their heads. I have also tried making my own paper patterns, to work out how to make bears that look a bit different, like my Long Necked Ladies and my Zebra Noses. Once I gave a bear as a present to the Taiwan poet Ya Hsien. With his usual sense of poetic uncertainty he said: 'Is this really a bear? Why isn't it like other bears?' In the end you just have to put your doubts to one side. Maybe it's something to do with age, but I personally don't really like those kitsch teddies trying to look 'cute'.

Ho: The outlaws from *Water Margin* are so cute though, their brilliance lies in the way they look so innocent and pure, but still so witty.

Xi: Just imagine if I had made them into pirates! They wouldn't have looked any good as some holy do-gooders, either. You know, real bears would hardly ever look their opponent in the eye. It's a sure sign of bad intentions. Well at the very least, there's nothing friendly about it.

Ho: These outlaws from *Water Margin* are different to the Chinese Bears in Antique Garb.

Xi: A few years ago I was constantly searching for ways to make them stand up, so I could get them into character and show their personalities. Making the Antique Garb series was a big step. Bears have pads for walking, which means they walk on the 'palms' of their feet rather than on their toes. They can also use their hind legs only to get up. Some bears can actually make you jump with fright just by standing up. They suddenly appear to have grown a lot taller.

Ho: Through your teddy bears you introduce readers to ancient Chinese fashion.

Xi: Yes. I'm interested in the development of Chinese fashion, from remote antiquity right up to the Qing Dynasty. I selected a few famous people from each period. But it's not a formal history of Chinese clothing, because I've only included those characters I personally find interesting. The ones I happen to like can hardly be said to representatives of each dynasty in Chinese history.

Ho: The impulse for every major shift in Han Chinese clothing seems to have come from other nationalities. Some of these changes were implemented by the Han Chinese themselves, while others were imposed upon them. The first instance was Prince Wuling of Zhao in the Warring States period who adopted the northern style to be more comfortable on horseback and doing archery. The next major change came in the Wei, Jin, and Southern and Northern Dynasties.

Xi: Then came the Tang Dynasty with its mixture of different cultures, and after that came the Manchu Qing, which brought in a whole range of subtle, minute changes.

Afterword

After five years making teddy bears, complete with outfits, I just wanted to bring out a book with pictures of them to keep as a souvenir. Having pictures means someone has to take photographs. My elder brother is a professional, so I asked him to help me with that. He said, these days we all have our own digital cameras, which make things easy; it would be fine if you took the photos yourself. I believed him. Each time I finished two or three bears, I'd get out my digital camera and take a few shots. Later, my right hand lost feeling and really wasn't up to the task, so I approached my neighbour Ho Fuk-yan for help. He knew this way was quite amateur. Published books have to be careful with printing, so the photographs going into books need to take things like lighting, background, and depth of field into account. When the art editor saw the photographs of the bears, Ho Fuk-yan's were all right, but mine looked like they were on ecstasy! Luckily two angels came to the rescue, one was Mark Chan, the other was Lam Kwok-wai. They helped me carry several red-white-blue Hong Kong bags of teddy bears up to a studio with formal lighting and backdrops. They arranged everything and took some professional shots. All the wonderful pictures on display here are theirs. Thanks very much.

Of course I must thank Ho Fuk-yan for his preface,[50] his help with organising things, and his proofreading work. Thanks also to his elder brother Mr Frank Ho, who carved two beautiful seals for me. Thanks to my bear-making teacher, Miss Gloria Chan for her guidance. The big eyed bears were her idea. Of course I must also thank Sophie Choi and Amanda Woo from Joint Publishing for all the hard work they put into the design and editing of this book.[51]

Xi Xi
July 2009

---

50 Ho Fuk-yan wrote a preface for the original Chinese version that has not been included here.

51 This English translation is based on the 2009 Joint Publishing (Hong Kong) edition.

Bear Height Measurements

Chinese Bears in Antique Garb 38cm/ Hua Mulan 38cm/ Heroes from *Water Margin* 30cm/ Fancy Dress Ball 37cm/ Clan of the Zebra Noses 30cm/ Yellow Flying Bear 18cm/ Acrobats 18cm/ Giving Flowers 30cm/ Scarf Faction 36cm/ Long Necked Ladies 39cm/ Big Eyed Bears 18cm/ Injured Moon Bear 37cm/ Bear Friends 36cm (Bear with Claws, Floral Bear and Flannel Bear 38cm)/ Memorial Bear 37cm.

HONG KONG LITERATURE SERIES

Series Editor: John Minford

The Drunkard: A Novel by Liu Yichang
By Liu Yichang
Translated by Charlotte Chun-lam Yiu
Edited with an Introduction and Notes by Nick Hordern
978-988-237-186-6

Dragons: Shorter Fiction of Leung Ping-kwan
By Leung Ping-kwan
Translated by Wendy Chan, Jasmine Tong Man and David Morgan
Edited by Laura Ng and John Minford
978-988-237-190-3

Lotus Leaves: Selected Poems of Leung Ping-kwan
By Leung Ping-kwan
Translated and edited by John Minford
978-988-237-191-0

The Teddy Bear Chronicles
By Xi Xi
Translated by Christina Sanderson
978-988-237-185-9

Ordinary Days: A Memoir in Six Chapters
By Leo Ou-fan Lee and Esther Yuk-ying Lee
With a Preface by Pai Hsien-yung
Translated by Carol Ong and Annie Ren
Edited by John Minford
978-988-237-196-5

The Best China: Essays from Hong Kong
Edited and Translated by John Minford
978-988-237-197-2